Developing with PDF

Leonard Rosenthol

Beijing · Cambridge · Farnham · Köln · Sebastopol · Tokyo

Developing with PDF

by Leonard Rosenthol

Published by O'Reilly Media, Inc., 1005 Gravenstein Highway North, Sebastopol, CA 95472.

O'Reilly books may be purchased for educational, business, or sales promotional use. Online editions are also available for most titles (*http://my.safaribooksonline.com*). For more information, contact our corporate/institutional sales department: 800-998-9938 or *corporate@oreilly.com*.

Editors: Simon St. Laurent and Meghan Blanchette	**Cover Designer:** Randy Comer
Production Editor: Nicole Shelby	**Interior Designer:** David Futato
Copyeditor: Rachel Head	**Illustrator:** Rebecca Demarest
Indexer: WordCo Indexing Services	

October 2013:   First Edition

Revision History for the First Edition:

2013-10-11:   First release

See *http://oreilly.com/catalog/errata.csp?isbn=9781449327910* for release details.

ISBN: 978-1-449-32791-0

[LSI]

Table of Contents

Preface

The Portable Document Format (PDF) is the way in which most documents are produced for distribution, collaboration, and archiving worldwide. It has been standardized by the International Organization for Standardization (ISO) and by governments in over 75 countries as their format of choice for their documentation. The printing industry has required the use of PDF for any professional printing job. With billions of publicly available documents and an untold number of documents living in private repositories, no other file format has the wide reach and ubiquity that PDF does.

However, even with those billions of documents in circulation, the PDF format remains poorly understood by users and developers alike due to there being a dearth of documentation beyond ISO 32000-1, the PDF standard itself. And while the standard is an excellent technical document, its size, complexity, and dry style make it unapproachable for many.

The goal of this book is to provide an approachable reference to PDF. It covers key topics from the standard in a way that will enable the technically minded to understand what is inside a PDF. For those simply needing to examine the internals of a PDF to diagnose problems, you will find the tools you need here, and those who want to construct their own valid and well-formed documents will find out how to do so.

Who Should Read This Book

While this book goes into some fairly deep technical topics, I've tried to present them in such a way that any technically minded individual should find the material approachable and understandable.

This book is suitable for:

- Users of PDF software, such as Adobe Acrobat, who want to understand what is going on "under the hood" of the various features in those products (features like inserting and deleting pages or converting images).

- Industry professionals in areas such as electronic publishing and printing who want to better understand PDF in order to improve their systems, or who need to diagnose issues in their PDF processing.

- Programmers writing code to read, edit, or create PDF files.

Organization of Content

Chapter 1

We begin by looking at the various objects that make up a PDF file and how they are combined together into a cohesive whole.

Chapter 2

In this chapter we look at the core aspect of PDF—its imaging model. We learn how to create a page and draw some graphics on it.

Chapter 3

Continuing on from our discussion of the core imaging model, in this chapter we explore how to incorporate raster images into your PDF content.

Chapter 4

Next, we learn how to incorporate the last of the common types of PDF content—text. Of course, a discussion of text in PDF wouldn't be complete without an understanding of fonts and glyphs.

Chapter 5

PDF isn't just about static content. This chapter will introduce various ways in which a PDF can gain interactivity, specifically around enabling navigation within and between documents.

Chapter 6

This chapter explores the special objects that are *annotations*, which are drawn on top of the regular content to enable everything from interactive links to 3D to video and audio.

Chapter 7

Next, we look at how interactive forms are provided for in the PDF language.

Chapter 8

This chapter demonstrates how a PDF can be used in a way similar to a ZIP archive by embedding files inside of it.

Chapter 9

This chapter explains how video and audio content can be referenced in or embedded into a PDF for playing as part of rich content.

Chapter 10

This chapter introduces optional content, which only appears at certain times, such as on the screen but not when printed or only for certain users.

Chapter 11

This chapter looks at how to add semantic richness to your content by tagging it with HTML-like structures such as paragraphs and tables.

Chapter 12

This chapter explores the various ways in which metadata can be incorporated into a PDF file, from the simplest document level strings to rich XML attached to individual objects.

Chapter 13

Finally, this chapter introduces the various open international standards based on PDF, including the full PDF standard itself (ISO 32000-1), the various subsets (such as PDF/A and PDF/X), as well as related work (such as PAdES).

Conventions Used in This Book

The following typographical conventions are used in this book:

Italic

Indicates new terms, URLs, email addresses, file and path names, and file extensions.

`Constant width`

Used for program listings, as well as within paragraphs to refer to program elements such as variable or function names, operators and operands, HTML elements, and keys and their values.

This icon signifies a tip, suggestion, or general note.

This icon indicates a warning or caution.

Safari® Books Online

Safari Books Online is an on-demand digital library that delivers expert content in both book and video form from the world's leading authors in technology and business.

Technology professionals, software developers, web designers, and business and creative professionals use Safari Books Online as their primary resource for research, problem solving, learning, and certification training.

Safari Books Online offers a range of product mixes and pricing programs for organizations, government agencies, and individuals. Subscribers have access to thousands of books, training videos, and prepublication manuscripts in one fully searchable database from publishers like O'Reilly Media, Prentice Hall Professional, Addison-Wesley Professional, Microsoft Press, Sams, Que, Peachpit Press, Focal Press, Cisco Press, John Wiley & Sons, Syngress, Morgan Kaufmann, IBM Redbooks, Packt, Adobe Press, FT Press, Apress, Manning, New Riders, McGraw-Hill, Jones & Bartlett, Course Technology, and dozens more. For more information about Safari Books Online, please visit us online.

How to Contact Us

Please address comments and questions concerning this book to the publisher:

O'Reilly Media, Inc.
1005 Gravenstein Highway North
Sebastopol, CA 95472
800-998-9938 (in the United States or Canada)
707-829-0515 (international or local)
707-829-0104 (fax)

We have a web page for this book, where we list errata, examples, and any additional information. You can access this page at *http://oreil.ly/developing-with-pdf*.

To comment or ask technical questions about this book, send email to *bookquestions@oreilly.com*.

For more information about our books, courses, conferences, and news, see our website at *http://www.oreilly.com*.

Find us on Facebook: *http://facebook.com/oreilly*

Follow us on Twitter: *http://twitter.com/oreillymedia*

Watch us on YouTube: *http://www.youtube.com/oreillymedia*

Acknowledgments

This book wouldn't exist were it not for the love and support of my בּאַשערט (bashert),
Marla Rosenthol.

Dr. James King and Dr. Matthew Hardy of Adobe Systems and Olaf Drümmer of Callas
Software took time out of their normal jobs to do technical reviews of the material in
this book. Thanks guys!

I would also like to thank my editors, Simon St. Laurent and Meghan Blanchette.

CHAPTER 1

PDF Syntax

We'll begin our exploration of PDF by diving right into the building blocks of the PDF file format. Using these blocks, you'll see how a PDF is constructed to lead to the page-based format that you are familiar with.

PDF Objects

The core part of a PDF file is a collection of "things" that the PDF standard (ISO 32000) refers to as *objects*, or sometimes *COS objects*.

 COS stands for Carousel Object System and refers to the original/ code name for Adobe's Acrobat product.

These aren't objects in the "object-oriented programming" sense of the word; instead, they are the building blocks on which PDF stands. There are nine types of objects: null, Boolean, integer, real, name, string, array, dictionary, and stream.

Let's look at each of these object types and how they are serialized into a PDF file. From there, you'll then see how to take these object types and use them to build higher-level constructs and the PDF format itself.

Null Objects

The null object, if actually written to a file, is simply the four characters *null*. It is synonymous with a missing value, which is why it's extremely rare to see one in a PDF. If you have reason to work with the null value, be sure to consult ISO 32000 carefully about the subtleties involving its handling.

Boolean Objects

Boolean objects represent the logical values of true and false and are represented accordingly in the PDF, either as true or false.

When writing a PDF, you will always use true or false. However, if you are reading/parsing a PDF and wish to be tolerant, be aware that poorly written PDFs may use other capitalization forms, including leading caps (True or False) or all caps (TRUE or FALSE).

Numeric Objects

PDF supports two different types of numeric objects—integer and real—representing their mathematical equivalents. While older versions of PDF had stated implementation limits that matched Adobe's older implementations, those should no longer be taken to be file format limitations (nor should those of any specific implementation by any vendor).

While PDF supports 64-bit numbers (so as to enable very large files), you will find that most PDFs don't actually need them. However, if you are reading a PDF, you may indeed encounter them, so be prepared.

Integer numeric objects consist of one or more decimal digits optionally preceded by a sign, representing a signed value (in base 10). Example 1-1 shows a few examples of integers.

Example 1-1. Integers

```
1
-2
+100
612
```

Real numeric objects consist of one or more decimal digits with an optional sign and a leading, trailing, or embedded period representing a signed real value. Unlike PostScript, PDF does not support scientific/exponential format, nor does it support non-decimal radices.

While the term "real" is used in PDF to represent the object type, the actual implementation of a given viewer might use *double*, *float*, or even *fixed point* numbers. Since the implementations may differ, the number of decimal places of precision may also differ. It is therefore recommended for reliability and also for file size considerations to not write more than four decimal places.

Example 1-2 shows some examples of what real numbers look like in PDF.

Example 1-2. Reals

```
0.05
.25
-3.14159
300.9001
```

Name Objects

A name object in PDF is a unique sequence of characters (except character code 0, ASCII null) normally used in situations where there is a fixed set of values. Names are written into a PDF with a / (SOLIDUS) character followed by a UTF-8 string, with a special encoding form for any nonregular character. Nonregular characters are those defined to be outside the range of 0x21 (!) through 0x7E (~), as well as any white-space character (see Table 1-1). These nonregular characters are encoded starting with a # (NUMBER SIGN) and then the two-digit hexadecimal code for the character.

Because of their unique nature, most names that you will write into a PDF are predefined in ISO 32000 or will be derived from external data (such as a font or color name).

If you need to create your own nonexternal data-based custom names (such as a private piece of metadata), you must follow the rules for *second class names* as defined in ISO 32000-1:2008, Annex E, if you wish your file to be considered a valid PDF. A second class name is one that begins with your four-character ISO-registered prefix followed by an underscore (_) and then the key name. An example is included at the end of Example 1-3.

Example 1-3. Names

```
/Type
/ThisIsName37
/Lime#20Green
/SSCN_SomeSecondClassName
```

String Objects

Strings as they are serialized into PDF are simply series of (zero or more) 8-bit bytes written either as literal characters enclosed in parentheses, (and), or hexadecimal data enclosed in angle brackets (< and >).

A literal string consists of an arbitrary number of 8-bit characters enclosed in parentheses. Because any 8-bit value may appear in the string, the unbalanced parentheses ( )) and the backslash (\) are treated specially through the use of the backslash to escape special values. Additionally, the backslash can be used with the special \ddd notation to specify other character values.

Literal strings come in a few different varieties:

ASCII
> A sequence of bytes containing only ASCII characters

PDFDocEncoded
> A sequence of bytes encoded according to the PDFDocEncoding (ISO 32000–1:2008, 7.9.2.3)

Text
> A sequence of bytes encoded as either the PDFDocEncoding or as UTF–16BE (with the leading byte order marker)

Date
> An ASCII string whose format D:YYYYMMDDHHmmSSOHH'mm is described in ISO 32000–1:2008, 7.9.4

 Dates, as a type of string, were added to PDF in version 1.1.

A series of hexadecimal digits (0–9, A–F) can be written between angle brackets, which is useful for including more human-readable arbitrary binary data or Unicode values (UCS-2 or UCS-4) in a string object. The number of digits must always be even, though white-space characters may be added between pairs of digits to improve human readability. Example 1-4 shows a few examples of strings in PDF.

Example 1-4. Strings

```
(Testing)                    % ASCII
(A\053B)                     % Same as (A+B)
(Français)                   % PDFDocEncoded
<FFFE0040>                   % Text with leading BOM
(D:19990209153925-08'00')    % Date
<1C2D3F>                     % Arbitrary binary data
```

The percent sign (%) denotes a comment; any text that follows it is ignored.

The previous discussion about strings was about how the values are serialized into a PDF file, not necessarily how they are handled internally by a PDF processor. While such internal handling is outside the scope of the standard, it is important to remember that different file serializations can produce the same internal representation (like (A \053B) and (A+B) in Example 1-4).

Array Objects

An array object is a heterogeneous collection of other objects enclosed in square brackets ([and]) and separated by white space. You can mix and match any objects of any type together in a single array, and PDF takes advantage of this in a variety of places. An array may also be empty (i.e., contain zero elements).

While an array consists only of a single dimension, it is possible to construct the equivalent of a multidimensional array. This construct is not used often in PDF, but it does appear in a few places, such as the Order array in a data structure known as an optional content group dictionary. (See "Optional Content Groups" on page 151.)

There is no limit to the number of elements in a PDF array. However, if you find an alternative to a large array (such as the page tree for a single Kids array), it is always better to avoid them for performance reasons.

Some examples of arrays are given in Example 1-5.

Example 1-5. Arrays

```
[ 0 0 612 792 ]           % 4-element array of all integers
[ (T) -20.5 (H) 4 (E) ]   % 5-element array of strings, reals, and integers
[ [ 1 2 3 ] [ 4 5 6 ] ]   % 2-element array of arrays
```

Dictionary Objects

As it serves as the basis for almost every higher-level object, the most common object in PDF is the dictionary object. It is a collection of key/value pairs, also known as an *associative table*. Each key is always a name object, but the value may be any other type of object, including another dictionary or even null.

When the value is null, it is treated as if the key is not present. There-fore, it is better to simply not write the key, to save processing time and file size.

A dictionary is enclosed in double angle brackets (<< and >>). Within those brackets, the keys may appear in any order, followed immediately by their values. Which keys appear in the dictionary will be determined by the definition (in ISO 32000) of the higher-level object that is being authored.

While many existing implementations tend to write the keys sorted alphabetically, that is neither required nor expected. In fact, no assumptions should be made about dictionary processing, either—the keys may be read and processed in any order. A dictionary that contains the same key twice is invalid, and which value is selected is undefined. Finally, while it improves human readability to put line breaks between key/value pairs, that too is not required and only serves to add bytes to the total file size.

There is no limit to the number of key/value pairs in a dictionary.

Example 1-6 shows a few examples.

Example 1-6. Dictionaries

```
% a more human-readable dictionary
<<
    /Type /Page
    /Author (Leonard Rosenthol)
    /Resources << /Font [ /F1 /F2 ] >>
>>

% a dictionary with all white-space stripped out
<</Length 3112/Subtype/XML/Type/Metadata>>
```

Name trees

A *name tree* serves a similar purpose to a dictionary, in that it provides a way to associate keys with values. However, unlike in a dictionary, the keys are string objects instead of names and are required to be ordered/sorted according to the standard Unicode collation algorithm (*http://www.unicode.org/reports/tr10/*).

This concept is called a name tree because there is a "root" dictionary (or node) that refers to one or more child dictionaries/nodes, which themselves can refer to one or more child dictionaries/nodes, thus creating many branches of a tree-like structure.

The root node holds a single key, either Names (for a simple tree) or Kids (for a more complex tree). In the case of a complex tree, each of the intermediate nodes will also have a Kids key present; the final/terminal nodes of each branch will contain the Names key. It is the array value of the Names key that specifies the keys and their values by alternating key/value, as shown in Example 1-7.

Example 1-7. Example name trees

```
% Simple name tree with just some names
1 0 obj
<<
    /Names    [
        (Apple)    (Orange)        % These are sorted, hence A, N, Z...
        (Name 1) 1                  % and values can be any type
        (Name 2) /Value2
        (Zebra) << /A /B >>
    ]
>>
endobj
```

Number trees

A *number tree* is similar to a name tree, except that its keys are integers instead of strings and are sorted in ascending numerical order. Also, the entries in the leaf (or root) nodes containing the key/value pairs are found as the value of the Nums key instead of the Names key.

Stream Objects

Streams in PDF are arbitrary sequences of 8-bit bytes that may be of unlimited length and can be compressed or encoded. As such, they are the object type used to store large blobs of data that are in some other standardized format, such as XML grammars, font files, and image data.

A stream object is represented by the data for the object preceded by a dictionary containing attributes of the stream and referred to as the *stream dictionary*. The use of the words stream (followed by an end-of-line marker) and endstream (preceded by an end-of-line marker) serve to delineate the stream data from its dictionary, while also differentiating it from a standard dictionary object. The stream dictionary never exists on its own; it is always a part of the stream object.

The stream dictionary always contains at least one key, Length, which represents the number of bytes from the beginning of the line following stream until the last byte before the end-of-the-line character preceding endstream. In other words, it is the actual number of bytes serialized into the PDF file. In the case of a compressed stream, it is the number of compressed bytes. Although not commonly provided, the original uncompressed length can be specified as the value of a DL key.

One of the most important keys that can be present in the stream dictionary is the `Filter` key, which specifies what (if any) compression or encoding was applied to the original data before it was included in the stream. It's quite common to compress large images and embedded fonts using the `FlateDecode` filter, which uses the same lossless compression technology used by the ZIP file format. For images, the two most common filters are `DCTDecode`, which produces a JPEG/JFIF-compatible stream, and `JPXDecode`, which produces a JPEG2000-compatible stream. Other filters can be found in ISO 32000-12008, Table 6. Example 1-8 shows what a steam object in PDF might look like.

Example 1-8. An example stream

```
<<
    /Type       /XObject
    /Subtype    /Image
    /Filter     /FlateDecode
    /Length     496
    /Height     32
    /Width      32
>>

stream
% 496 bytes of Flate-encoded data goes here...
endstream
```

Direct versus Indirect Objects

Now that you've been introduced to the types of objects, it is important to understand that these objects can be represented either directly or indirectly in the PDF.

Direct objects are those objects that appear "inline" and are obtained directly (hence the name) when the objects are being read from the file. They are usually found as the value of a dictionary key or an entry in an array and are the type of object that you've seen in all of the examples so far.

Indirect objects are those that are referred to (indirectly!) by reference and a PDF reader will have to jump around the file to find the actual value. In order to identify which object is being referred to, every indirect object has a unique (per-PDF) ID, which is expressed as a positive number, and a generation number, which is always a nonnegative number and usually zero (0). These numbers are used both to define the object and to reference the object.

 While originally intended to be used as a way to track revisions in PDF, generation numbers are almost never used by modern PDF systems, so they are almost always zero.

To use an indirect object, you must first define it using the ID and generation along with the `obj` and `endobj` keywords, as shown in Example 1-9.

Example 1-9. Indirect objects made entirely from direct objects

```
3 0 obj          % object ID 3, generation 0
<<
 /ProcSet [ /PDF /Text /ImageC /ImageI ]
 /Font <<
     /F1 <<
        /Type /Font
        /Subtype /Type1
        /Name /F1
        /BaseFont/Helvetica
        >>
     >>
>>
endobj

5 0 obj
(an indirect string)
endobj

% an indirect number
4 0 obj
1234567890
endobj
```

When you refer to an indirect object, you do so using its ID, its generation, and the character R. For example, it's quite common to see something like Example 1-10, where two indirect objects (IDs 4 and 5) are referenced.

Example 1-10. An indirect object that references other indirect objects

```
3 0 obj                 % object ID 3, generation 0
<<
 /ProcSet 5 0 R         % reference the indirect object with ID 5, generation 0
 /Font <</F1 4 0 R >>   % reference the indirect object with ID 4, generation 0
>>
endobj
4 0 obj                 % object ID 4, generation 0
<<
 /Type /Font
 /Subtype /Type1
 /Name /F1
 /BaseFont/Helvetica
>>
endobj
5 0 obj                 % object ID 5, generation 0
[ /PDF /Text /ImageC /ImageI ]
endobj
```

By using a combination of ID and generation, each object can be uniquely identified inside of a given PDF. Using the cross-reference table feature of PDF, each indirect object can easily be located and loaded on demand from the reference.

 Unless otherwise indicated by ISO 32000, any time you use an object it can be of either type—except for streams, which can only be indirect.

File Structure

If you were to view a simple PDF file—let's call it *Hello World.pdf*—in a PDF viewer, it would look like Figure 1-1.

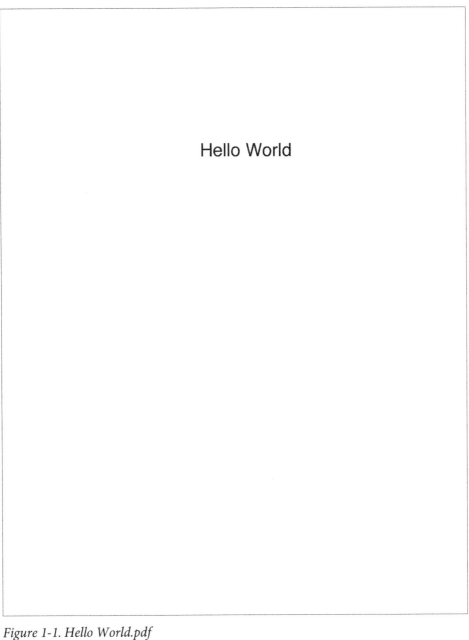

Hello World

Figure 1-1. Hello World.pdf

But if you were to view *Hello World.pdf* in a text editing application, it would look something like Example 1-11.

Example 1-11. What "Hello World.pdf" looks like in a text editor

```
%PDF-1.4
%%EOF

6 0 obj
<<
 /Type /Catalog
 /Pages 5 0 R
>>
endobj

1 0 obj
<<
 /Type /Page
 /Parent 5 0 R
 /MediaBox [ 0 0 612 792 ]
 /Resources 3 0 R
 /Contents 2 0 R
>>
endobj

4 0 obj
<<
 /Type /Font
 /Subtype /Type1
 /Name /F1
 /BaseFont/Helvetica
>>
endobj

2 0 obj
<<
 /Length 53
>>
stream
BT
 /F1 24 Tf
 1 0 0 1 260 600 Tm
 (Hello World)Tj
ET
endstream
endobj

5 0 obj
<<
 /Type /Pages
 /Kids [ 1 0 R ]
 /Count 1
>>
endobj

3 0 obj
```

```
<<
 /ProcSet[/PDF/Text]
 /Font <</F1 4 0 R >>
>>
endobj

xref
0 7
0000000000 65535 f
0000000060 00000 n
0000000228 00000 n
0000000424 00000 n
0000000145 00000 n
0000000333 00000 n
0000000009 00000 n
trailer
<<
 /Size 7
 /Root 6 0 R
>>
startxref
488
%%EOF
```

Looking at that, you might get the mistaken impression that a PDF file is a text file that can be routinely edited using a text editor—it is *not*! A PDF file is a structured 8-bit binary document delineated by a series of 8-bit character-based tokens, separated by white space and arranged into (arbitrarily long) lines. These tokens serve not only to delineate the various objects and their types, as you saw in the previous section, but also to define where the four logical sections of the PDF begin and end. (See Figure 1-2.)

As noted previously, the tokens in a PDF are always encoded (and therefore decoded) as 8-bit bytes in ASCII. They cannot be encoded in any other way, such as Unicode. Of course, specific data or object values can be encoded in Unicode; we'll discuss those cases as they arise.

White-Space

The white-space characters shown in Table 1-1 are used in PDF to separate syntactic constructs such as names and numbers from each other.

Table 1-1. White-space characters

Decimal	Hexadecimal	Octal	Name
0	00	000	NULL (NUL)
9	09	011	HORIZONTAL TAB (HT)

Decimal	Hexadecimal	Octal	Name
10	0A	012	LINE FEED (LF)
12	0C	014	FORM FEED (FF)
13	0D	015	CARRIAGE RETURN (CR)
32	20	040	SPACE (SP)

In all contexts except comments, strings, cross-reference table entries, and streams, PDF treats any sequence of consecutive white-space characters as one character.

The CARRIAGE RETURN (*0Dh*) and LINE FEED (*0Ah*) characters, also called *newline characters*, are treated as end-of-line (EOL) markers. The combination of a CARRIAGE RETURN followed immediately by a LINE FEED is treated as one EOL marker. EOL markers are typically treated the same as any other white-space characters. However, sometimes an EOL marker is required, preceding a token that appears at the beginning of a line.

The Four Sections of a PDF

Figure 1-2 illustrates the four sections of a PDF: the header, trailer, body, and cross-reference table.

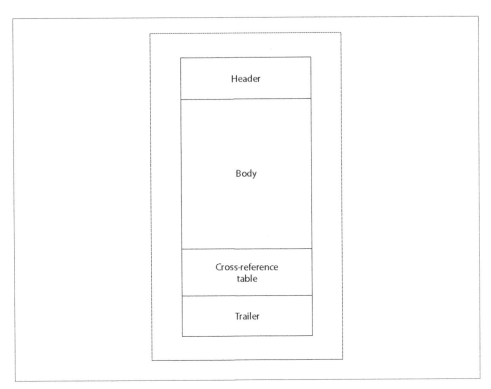

Figure 1-2. The four sections of a PDF

Header

The header of a PDF starts at byte 0 of the file and consists of at least 8 bytes followed by an end-of-line marker. These 8 bytes serve to clearly identify that the file is a PDF (*%PDF-*) and suggest a version number of the standard that the file complies with (e.g., 1.4). If your PDF contains actual binary data (and these days, pretty much all of them do) a second line will follow, which also starts with the PDF comment character, % (PERCENT SIGN). Following the % on the second line will be at least four characters whose ASCII values are greater than 127. Although any four (or more) values are fine, the most commonly used are *âãÏÓ* (0xE2E3CFD3).

 The second line is there to trick programs that do ASCII vs. binary detection by simply counting high-order ASCII values. Including those values ensures that PDFs will always be considered as binary.

Trailer

At the opposite end of the PDF from the header, one can find the trailer. A simple example is shown in Example 1-12. The trailer is primarily a dictionary with keys and values that provides document-level information that is necessary to understand in order to process the document itself.

Example 1-12. A simple trailer

```
trailer
<<
 /Size 23
 /Root 5 0 R
 /ID[<E3FEB541622C4F35B45539A690880C71><E3FEB541622C4F35B45539A690880C71>]
 /Info 6 0 R
>>
```

The two most important keys, and the only two that are required, are Size and Root. The Size key tells us how many entries you should expect to find in the cross-reference table that precedes the trailer dictionary. The Root key has as its value the document's catalog dictionary, which is where you will start in order to find all the objects in the PDF.

Other common keys in the trailer are the Encrypt key, whose presence quickly identifies that a given PDF has been encrypted; the ID key, which provides two unique IDs for the document; and the Info key, which represents the original method of providing document-level metadata (this has been replaced, as described in Chapter 12).

Body

The body is where all the nine types of objects that comprise the actual document itself are located in the file. You will see more about this in "Document Structure" on page 21 as you look at the various objects and how they are organized.

Cross-reference table

The cross-reference table is simple in concept and implementation, but it is one of the core attributes of PDF. This table provides the binary offset from the beginning of the file for each and every indirect object in the file, allowing a PDF processor to quickly seek to and then read any object at any time. This model for random access means that a PDF can be opened and processed quickly, without having to load the entire document into memory. Additionally, navigation between pages is quick, regardless of how large the "numeric jump" in the page numbers is. Having the cross-reference table at the end of the file also provides two additional benefits: creation of the PDF in a single pass (no backtracking) is possible, and support for incremental updates of the document is facilitated (see "Incremental Update" on page 18 for an example).

The original form (from PDF 1.0 to 1.4) of the cross-reference table is comprised of one or more cross-reference sections, where each of these sections is a series of entries (one line per object) with the object's file offset, its generation, and whether it is still in use. The most common type of table, shown in Figure 1-3, has only a single section listing all objects.

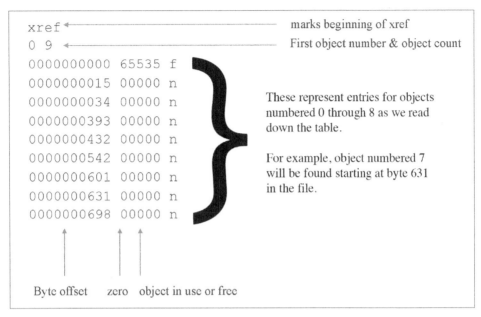

```
xref                           marks beginning of xref
0 9                            First object number & object count
0000000000 65535 f
0000000015 00000 n
0000000034 00000 n            These represent entries for objects
0000000393 00000 n            numbered 0 through 8 as we read
0000000432 00000 n            down the table.
0000000542 00000 n
0000000601 00000 n            For example, object numbered 7
0000000631 00000 n            will be found starting at byte 631
0000000698 00000 n            in the file.


Byte offset    zero   object in use or free
```

Figure 1-3. Classic cross-reference table

This type of cross-reference table follows a very rigid format where the column positions are fixed and the zeros are required.

You may notice that the values of the numbers in the second column of each line of the cross-reference table are always zero, except for the first one, which is 65535. That value, combined with the f, gives the clear indication that the object with that ID is not valid. Since a PDF file may never have an object of ID 0, that first line always looks the way you see it in this example.

However, when a PDF contains an incremental update, you may see a cross-reference section that looks like the one in Example 1-13.

Example 1-13. Updated cross-reference section

```
xref
0 1
0000000000 65535 f
4 1
```

```
0000000000 00001 f
6 2
0000014715 00000 n
0000018902 00000 n
10 1
0000019077 00000 n
trailer
<</Size 18/Root 9 0 R/Prev 14207
/ID[<86E7D6BF23F4475FB9DEED829A563FA7><507D41DDE6C24F52AC1EE1328E44ED26>]>>
```

As PDF documents became larger, it was clear that having this very verbose (and un-compressable) format was a problem that needed addressing. Thus, with PDF 1.5, a new type of cross-reference storage system called *cross-reference streams* (because the data is stored as a standard stream object) was introduced. In addition to being able to be compressed, the new format is more compact and supports files that are greater than 10 gigabytes in size, while also providing for other types of future expansion (that have not yet been utilized). In addition to moving the cross-reference table to a stream, this new system also made it possible to store collections of indirect objects inside of another special type of stream called an *object stream*. By intelligently splitting the objects among multiple streams, it is possible to optimize the load time and/or memory consumption for the PDF. Example 1-14 shows what a cross-reference stream looks like.

Example 1-14. Inside a cross-reference stream

```
stream
01 0E8A 0      % Entry for object 2 (0x0E8A = 3722)
02 0002 00     % Entry for object 3 (in object stream 2, index 0)
02 0002 01     % Entry for object 4 (in object stream 2, index 1)
02 0002 02     % . . .
02 0002 03
02 0002 04
02 0002 05
02 0002 06
02 0002 07     % Entry for object 10 (in object stream 2, index 7)
01 1323 0      % Entry for object 11 (0x1323 = 4899)
endstream
```

Incremental Update

As mentioned earlier, one of the key features of PDF that was made possible through the use of a trailer and cross-reference table at the end of the document is the concept of *incremental update*. Since changed objects are written to the end of the PDF, as il-lustrated in Figure 1-4, saving modifications is very quick as there is no need to read and process every object.

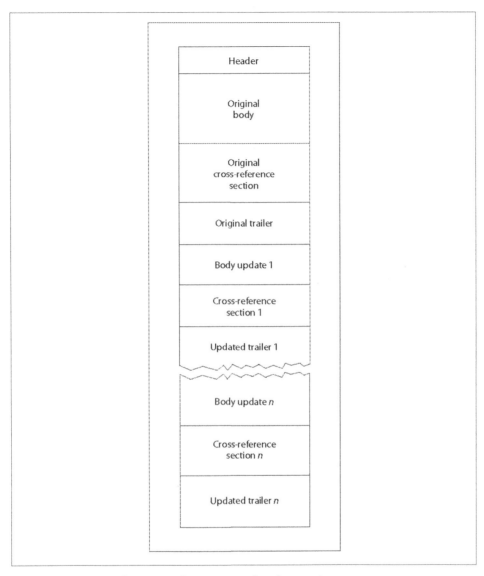

Figure 1-4. Layout of a PDF with incremental update sections

Each cross-reference section after the first points backward to the cross-reference section that preceded it via the Prev key in the trailer dictionary (see "Trailer" on page 16), and then only lists the new, changed, or deleted objects in the new table, as seen in Example 1-13.

Although viewers don't actually offer this feature (except after a digital signature, like in "Signature Fields" on page 119, has been applied), the use of incremental updates means that it is possible to support multiple undos across save boundaries. However, that also brings dangers from people who are looking through your (uncollected) garbage. Even though you thought you deleted something from the file, it may still be there if an incremental update was applied instead of a full save.

 When incrementally updating a PDF, it is extremely important that you do not mix classic cross-references with cross-reference streams. Whatever type of cross-reference is used in the original must also be used in the update section(s). If you do mix them, a PDF reader may choose to ignore the updates.

Linearization

As you've seen, having the cross-reference table at the end of the file offers various advantages. However, there is also one large disadvantage, and that's when the PDF has to be read over a "streaming interface" such as an HTTP stream in a web browser. In that case, a normal PDF would have to be downloaded in its entirety before even a single page could be read—not a great user experience.

To address this, PDF provides a feature called *linearization* (ISO 32000-1:2008, Annex F), but better known as "Fast Web View."

A linearized file differs from a standard PDF in three ways:

1. The objects in the file are ordered in a special way, such that all of the objects for a particular page are grouped together and then organized in numerical page order (e.g., objects for page 1, then objects for page 2, etc.).

2. A special *linearization parameter dictionary* is present, immediately following the header, which identifies the file as being linearized and contains various information needed to process it as such.

3. A partial cross-reference table and trailer are placed at the beginning of the file to enable access to all objects needed by the Root object, plus those objects representing the first page to be displayed (usually 1).

Of course, as with a standard PDF, objects are still referenced in the same way, continuing to enable random access to any object through the cross-reference table. A fragment of a linearized PDF is shown in Example 1-15.

Example 1-15. Linearized PDF fragment

```
%PDF-1.7
%%EOF
8 0 obj
<</Linearized 1/L 7546/O 10/E 4079/N 1/T 7272/H [ 456 176]>>
endobj
```

```
xref
8 8
0000000016 00000 n
0000000632 00000 n
0000000800 00000 n
0000001092 00000 n
0000001127 00000 n
0000001318 00000 n
0000003966 00000 n
0000000456 00000 n
trailer
<</Size 16/Root 9 0 R/Info 7 0 R/ID[<568899E9010A45B5A30E98293
C6DCD1D><068A37E2007240EF9D346D00AD08F696>]/Prev 7264>>
startxref
0
%%EOF

% body objects go here...
```

 Mixing linearization and incremental updates can yield unexpected results, since the linearized cross-reference table will be used instead of the updated versions, which only exist at the end of the file. Therefore, it is important that files destined for use online should be fully saved, to remove updates and ensure the correct linearization tables.

Document Structure

Now that you've learned about the various objects in the PDF and how they are put together to form the physical file layout/structure, it's time to put them together to form an actual document.

The Catalog Dictionary

A PDF document is a collection of objects, starting with the Root object (Figure 1-5). The reason that it is called the root is that if you think of the objects in a PDF as a tree (or a directed graph), this object is at the root of the tree/graph. From this object, you can find all the other objects that are needed to process the pages of the PDF and their content.

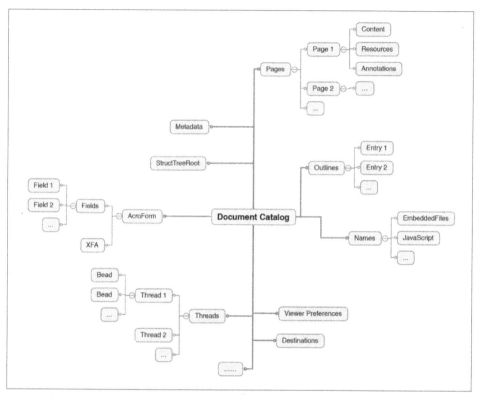

Figure 1-5. Graph-like structure of PDF objects

The Root is always an object of type Catalog and is known as the document's *catalog dictionary*. It has two required keys:

1. Type, whose value will always be the name object Catalog
2. Pages, whose value is an indirect reference to the page tree ("The Page Tree" on page 24)

While being able to get to the pages of the PDF is obviously important, there are over two dozen optional keys that can also be present (see ISO 32000-1:2008, Table 28). These represent document-level information including such things as:

- XML-based metadata ("XMP" on page 179)
- OpenActions ("Actions" on page 79)
- Fillable forms (Chapter 7)
- Optional content (Chapter 10)

- Logical structure and tags (Chapter 11)

Example 1-16 shows an example of a catalog object.

Example 1-16. Catalog object

```
<<
    /Type /Catalog
    /Pages 533 0 R
    /Metadata 537 0 R
    /PageLabels 531 0 R
    /OpenAction 540 0 R
    /AcroForm 541 0 R
    /Names 542 0 R
    /PageLayout /SinglePage
    /ViewerPreferences << /DisplayDocTitle true >>
>>
```

Let's look at a few keys (and their values) that you may find useful to include in your PDFs in order to improve the user experience:

PageLayout

> The PageLayout key is used to tell the viewer how to display the PDF pages. Its value is a name object (see "Name Objects" on page 3). To display them one at a time, use a value of SinglePage, or if you want the pages all in a long continuous column, use a value of OneColumn. There are also values that can be specified for two pages at a time (sometimes called a *spread*), depending on where you want the odd-numbered pages to fall: TwoPageLeft and TwoPageRight.

PageMode

> In addition to just having the PDF page content displayed, you may wish to have some of the navigational elements of a PDF immediately accessible to the user. For example, you might want the bookmarks or outlines visible (see "Bookmarks or Outlines" on page 83 for more on these). The value of the PageMode key, which is a name object, determines what (if any) extra elements are shown, such as UseOut lines, UseThumbs, or UseAttachments.

ViewerPreferences

> Unlike the previous two examples, where the values of the keys were name objects, the ViewerPreferences key has a value that is a viewer preferences dictionary (see ISO 32000-1:2008, 12.2). Among the many keys available for use in the viewer preferences dictionary, the most important one to use (provided you add metadata to your document, as discussed in Chapter 12) is shown in the previous example: DisplayDocTitle. Having that present with a value of true instructs a PDF viewer to display not the document's filename in the title bar of the window, as shown in Figure 1-6, but rather its real title, as shown in Figure 1-7.

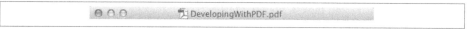

Figure 1-6. Window title bar showing the filename

Figure 1-7. Window title bar showing document title

The Page Tree

The pages in a PDF are accessed through the page tree, which defines the ordering of the pages. The page tree is usually implemented as a balanced tree but can also be just a simple array of pages.

> It is recommend that you have no more than about 25–50 pages in a single leaf of the tree. This means that any document larger than that should not be using a single array, but instead should be building a balanced tree. The reason for doing so is that the design of a balanced tree means that on devices with limited memory or resources, it is possible to find any specific page without having to load the entire array and then sequentially access each page in the array.

As you can see in Figure 1-8, there are two types of nodes in the page tree: intermediate nodes (of type Pages) and terminal or leaf nodes (of type Page). Intermediate nodes, which include the starting node of the tree, provide indirect references to their parents (if any) and children, along with a count of the leaf nodes in their particular branches of the tree. The leaf node is the actual Page object.

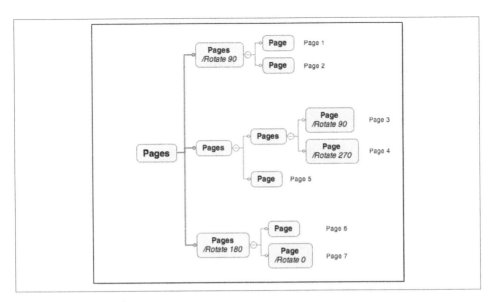

Figure 1-8. Image of a page tree

A portion of the Figure 1-8, represented in PDF syntax might look like Example 1-17.

Example 1-17. Objects making up a sample page tree

```
2 0 obj
<<
    /Type /Pages
    /Kids[ 4 0 R ]
    /Count 3
>>
endobj

4 0 obj
<<
    /Type /Pages
    /Parent 2 0 R
    /Rotate    90
    /Kids[ 5 0 R  6 0 R ]
    /Count 3
>>
endobj

5 0 obj
<<
    /Type /Page
    % Additional entries describing the attributes of Page 1
>>
endobj
```

```
6 0 obj
<<
    /Type /Page
    % Additional entries describing the attributes of Page 2
>>
endobj
```

Pages

As just discussed, each leaf node in the page tree represents a page object. The page object is a dictionary whose Type key has a value of Page; it also contains a few other required keys and may contain a dozen or more optional keys and their values.

Example 1-18 shows a few sample page dictionaries.

Example 1-18. Two sample page dictionaries

```
% simplest valid page object, with the four required keys
<<
    /Type /Page
    /Parent 2 0 R
    /MediaBox [ 0 0 612 792 ]     % Page Size == 8.5 x 11 in (612/72 x 792/72)
    /Resources <<>>
>>


% a real-world page object
<<
    /Type /Page
    /Parent 532 0 R
    /MediaBox [ 0 0 612 792 ]
    /CropBox [ 0 0 500 600 ]
    /Contents 564 0 R
    /Resources <<
        /ExtGState << /GS0 571 0 R /GS1 572 0 R >>
        /Font << /T1_0 566 0 R >>
        /XObject << /Im0 577 0 R >>
    >>
    /Trans << /S /Dissolve >>
    /Rotate 90
    /Annots 549 0 R
    /AA << /C 578 0 R /O 579 0 R >>
>>
```

There are a few keys to point out here, some of which we will delve into in future chapters:

Content

Unless you want blank pages in your PDF, this is the most important key in the page dictionary as it points to a content stream containing the instructions for what to draw on the page (see "Content Streams" on page 35).

Rotate

This key can be used to rotate the page in increments of 90 degrees. However, while a proper and valid part of PDF, it is frequently ignored by many lower-end tools. Therefore, consider using properly sized pages and (if necessary) transformed content, as described in "Transformations" on page 42.

Trans

If present, this key tells a viewer that when displaying the page in a "presentation style," it should use the defined transition when moving to this page from the one that precedes it. Details of the values for this key can be found in ISO 32000-1:2008, 12.4.4.

Annots

The value of this key is an array of all of the annotations (see Chapter 6) that are present on top of the page's content.

AA

Actions represent things that the viewer will do upon implicit actions by the user, such as opening or closing a page (see "Actions" on page 79 for more).

Resources

These are used to help complete the definitions of graphic objects, such as the font or color to use, that are necessary in order to draw on a page. They will be presented in the next chapter.

PDF units

Often when you work with graphic systems, you are working directly at the resolution of the output device, such as a 72 or 90 dpi (dots per inch) screen or a 600 dpi printer. This is referred to as *device space* (Figure 1-9).

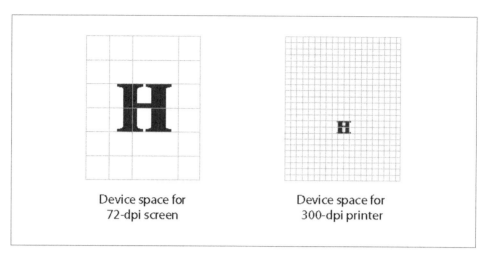

Figure 1-9. Device space

However, as this figure shows, if you want the same-sized object to appear regardless of the device's characteristics, you need to work in something other than device space. With PDF, that is called *user space*, and it stays the same regardless of the output device (Figure 1-10).

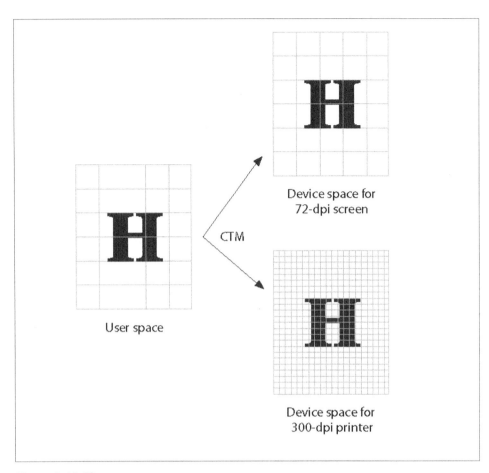

Figure 1-10. User space

User space defaults to 72 user units per inch (aka "points"), with the origin at the bottom left. It is possible to change the number of *user units* either through the use of a coordinate transform in the page content (see "Transformations" on page 42) or the presence of a UserUnit key in the page dictionary (as illustrated in Example 1-19). The origin of the coordinate system will always be [0 0], but that may not correspond to the bottom-left corner of the visible PDF page, depending on the values of the page boxes (see "Rects and boxes" on page 30).

Example 1-19. Example pages that use the UserUnit key

```
2 0 obj
<<
    /Type /Pages
    /Kids[ 3 0 R  4 0 R  5 0 R ]
    /Count 3
```

```
>>
endobj

3 0 obj
<<
    /Type /Page
    /Parent 2 0 R
    /UserUnit    1.0           % default of 72 units/inch
    /MediaBox [ 0 0 612 792 ]  % 8.5 x 11 inches
    % more keys here...
>>
endobj

4 0 obj
<<
    /Type /Page
    /Parent 2 0 R
    /UserUnit    2.0           % 144 units/inch (2 * 72)
    /MediaBox [ 0 0 612 792 ]  % 17 x 22 inches
    % more keys here...
>>
endobj

5 0 obj
<<
    /Type /Page
    /Parent 2 0 R
    /UserUnit    3.14159       % something funny but perfectly valid
    /MediaBox [ 0 0 612 792 ]  % 26.70 x 34.56 inches
    % more keys here...
>>
endobj
```

Rects and boxes

When describing a rectangle in PDF syntax, an array of four numbers is used. The order of the numbers is: left, bottom, width, height. You will find rects used in various places in PDF syntax, but the type of rect that you will be using most frequently is to define the sizes of various regions on a page—the *page boxes*.

Each of the five page boxes (ISO 32000-1:2008, 14.11.2) represents a rectangular viewing area (a "box") for the graphic elements that are drawn on the page, either directly or via annotations. The four numbers in the array are always in user units, the units of user space (see Figure 1-10. Since it represents a view into the coordinate system of the page, the rectangle need not have its bottom-left corner at [0 0].

The MediaBox of a page defines the size of the page on which the drawing will take place. Normally this is equivalent to a common paper size, such as *US Letter* (8.5 x 11 inches) or *A4* (21 x 29.7 cm), although it can be any size.

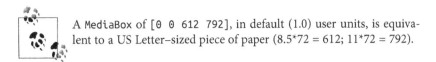 A MediaBox of [0 0 612 792], in default (1.0) user units, is equivalent to a US Letter–sized piece of paper (8.5*72 = 612; 11*72 = 792).

In addition to the MediaBox, there are four other page boxes that may appear on a page. They are shown in Figure 1-11.

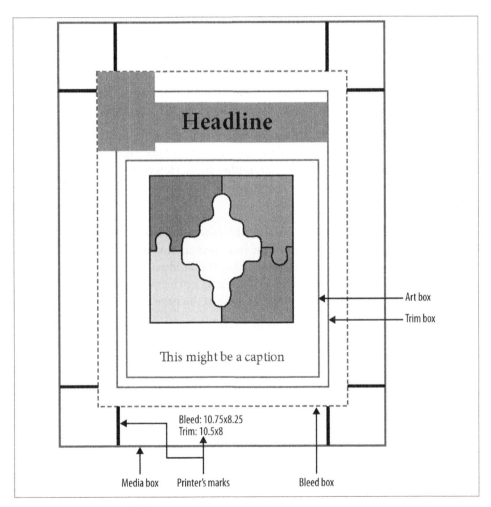

Figure 1-11. Page with boxes

A CropBox is used to instruct a PDF viewer of the actual visible area of the page when it is displayed or printed. This is primarily used when you have content on a page that you don't want a user to see, so you "crop" it out. Unlike in an image editor, applying a CropBox doesn't remove anything; it simply hides it outside the visible area.

 Although the CropBox may extend beyond the MediaBox, a PDF viewer will effectively pin the values to those of the MediaBox.

In the printing industry, a TrimBox serves a somewhat similar purpose. It defines where a cutter will trim (cut) the paper after it's been printed, thus removing content outside of the TrimBox from the final piece. It is used when you have something you want to come right up to the edge of the paper, without any white space or gap. For this to work, there is almost always a related BleedBox, which defines the area outside of the Trim Box where the content "bleeds" out so that it can be properly trimmed.

The final box, called the ArtBox, is almost never used. It was originally supposed to be used to represent an area that covered just the "artwork" of the page that one might use to repurpose, placing or imposing it onto another sheet. However, it never really caught on, and you should simply not bother using them in your documents.

Inheritance

As you saw in "Pages" on page 26, some of the values that would normally be present in a Page object can also be present in the intermediate nodes (Pages objects). When this happens, those values are inherited by all of the children of that node, unless they choose to override them. For example, if all the pages of a document are the same size, you could put the MediaBox key in the root node of the page tree.

Not all of the keys that can be present in a page object can be inherited, only those identified as such in ISO 32000-1:2008, Table 30.

 A linearized PDF cannot use inheritance. All values must be specified in each page object directly.

The Name Dictionary

Some types of objects in a PDF file can be referred to by name rather than by object reference. This correspondence between names and objects is established by using something called a document's *name dictionary*. The name dictionary is specified by including a Names key in the document's catalog dictionary (see "The Catalog Dictionary" on page 21). Each of the defined keys that can be present in this dictionary designates the root of a name tree that defines the names for that particular category of objects. Some of the types of objects that can be referenced by name are listed in Table 1-2:

Table 1-2. Some name dictionary entries

Key	Object type
Dests	Named destinations ("Named Destinations" on page 78)
AP	Appearance streams for annotations ("Appearance Streams" on page 88)
JavaScript	JavaScript files
EmbeddedFiles	Embedded files ("The EmbeddedFiles Name Tree" on page 127)

What's Next

In this chapter you learned about the basic syntax of PDF, starting from the basic types of objects and moving to the structure of a PDF file. You also learned about how these objects come together to form the document and its pages, and what keys can be found in a page object.

Next you'll learn about the PDF imaging model, content streams, and how to actually draw things on a page.

CHAPTER 2

PDF Imaging Model

In this chapter you'll begin your exploration into the PDF imaging model—that is, the various types of graphic operations that can be carried out on the pages of a document. You'll learn not only the language used to describe those operations, but also about various graphic and imaging concepts that accompany it.

Content Streams

As described in the previous chapter, a PDF file is composed of one or more pages (of a fixed size), and the visible elements on each page come from either the page content or a series of annotations that sit on top (visibly) of the content. This chapter discusses the page content.

Page content is described using a special text-based syntax (related to, but different from the PDF file syntax that you learned about in Chapter 1) that is stored in the PDF inside of a special type of stream object called a *content stream*. The content syntax is derived from Adobe's Postscript language and is comprised of a series of operators and their operands, where each operand can be expressed as a standard PDF object (see "PDF Objects" on page 1). A simple example, for drawing a rectangle filled with the color blue, is given in Example 2-1.

Example 2-1. Drawing a simple rectangle

```
0 0 1 rg           % set the color to blue in RGB
0 0 100 100 re     % draw a rectangle 100x100 with the bottom left at 0,0
F                  % fill it
```

We'll look at the various operators themselves shortly, but for now, the most important thing to take away from the example is that the syntax is expressed in Reverse Polish Notation, where the operator follows the operands (if any). The second thing you should remember about the page syntax language is that, unlike Postscript, it's not a true programming language in that it has no variables, loops, or conditional branching.

The content operators can be logically broken down into three categories. The most important ones, of course, are the drawing operators that cause something to be actually drawn onto the page. However, the drawing operators wouldn't be fully useful without the ability to set the attributes of the *graphic state* that defines how the drawing will look (such as the color or pen width). Finally, there are a set of operators called *marked content operators* that let you apply special properties to a group of operators.

Graphic State

As mentioned, drawing wouldn't be useful if you couldn't set all the attributes of the drawing. Thus, we'll start with the graphic state and its operators. You can think of the graphic state as a class or structure with members or properties and associated setters for changing the values. There are no getters, since there are no variables or conditionals in the content syntax to assign the values to or perform any operations on. This is extremely important, since it means that there isn't a direct means to change some values in the graphic state and then set them back to what they were previously. You might think this means you either need to draw all "like objects" together or do a lot of "resetting." Fortunately, you don't have to do either! A PDF processor is required to maintain a stack (in the traditional programming sense) of graphic state, that the content stream can push new states onto or pop completed states off of. This way, you can save the state, do something, then return to the previous state. The operators for doing this are *q* and *Q* (see Example 2-2).

Example 2-2. Drawing two rectangles

```
4 w                % set the line width to 4, for all objects
q                  % push/save the state
1 0 0 RG           % set the stroking color to red
0 0 100 100 re     % draw a rectangle 100x100 with bottom left at 0,0
```

```
S                       % stroke with a 4-unit width
Q                       % pop the state
q                       % push/save the state
0 1 0 RG                % set the stroking color to green
100 100 100 100 re      % draw a rectangle 100x100 with bottom left at 100,100
S                       % stroke with a 4-unit width
Q                       % pop the state
```

In this example, we used an operator that you hadn't seen before (w) to set the width of the pen in the graphic state. As you might imagine, this is a common operation.

Additionally, there are a few other types of attributes that you can set when working with lines (or stroking of any shape), including dash patterns and what happens when two lines connect or join. Example 2-3 is an example of drawing two dashed lines.

Example 2-3. Drawing dashed lines

```
8 w
q
    1 0 0 RG
    [5] 0 d         % simple 5 on, 5 off dash pattern
    100 100 m       % move to 100,100
    500 500 l       % draw a line to 500,500
    S
Q
q
    0 1 0 RG
    [5 10] 0 d      % 5 on, 10 of, dash pattern
    500 100 m       % move to 500,100
    100 500 l       % draw a line to 100,500
    S
Q
```

Example 2-4 shows the different types of line joins and caps (ends of a line).

Example 2-4. Various line joins and caps

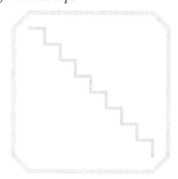

```
q
0 1 0 RG
10 w
1 j                         % set the line join to round
1 J                         % set the line cap to round
100 500 m
150 500 l
150 450 l
200 450 l
200 400 l
250 400 l
250 350 l
300 350 l
300 300 l
350 300 l
350 250 l
400 250 l
400 200 l
450 200 l
450 150 l
500 150 l
500 100 l
S
Q
q
0 1 1 RG
15 w
2 j                         % set the line join to bevel
50 500 m
100 550 l
500 550 l
550 500 l
550 100 l
500 50 l
100 50 l
50 100 l
```

```
        h                  % makes sure that the shape is a closed shape
        S
     Q
```

The Painter's Model

If you look at the previous examples, you'll see that the way you draw shapes (or *paths*, as they are called in PDF terms) is to first define or construct the path and then either stroke (S), fill, (F/f), or both (B) the path. Each path is drawn in the order that it appears in the content stream, in a form of "first in, first out" (FIFO) operation. What that means is that if you want to draw one path on top of another, you just draw it after. The combination of these two attributes is usually called the *Painter's Model*.

 The Painter's Model is also used by graphic systems such as SVG (*http://bit.ly/18FCE7r*) and Apple's Quartz 2D (*http://bit.ly/16PAltO*).

Example 2-5 illustrates how this works.

Example 2-5. Three overlapping rectangles

```
1 0 0 rg
209 426 -114 124 re
F
0 1 0 rg
237 401 -114 124 re
F
0 0 1 rg
272 373 -114 124 re
F
```

Open versus Closed Paths

Another aspect of the model is that shapes can be *open* or *closed*, which determines how the various stroking and filling operations complete when they reach the end of a path. Consider a path like the one in Example 2-6 that consists of a move to point A, then a line to point B, and another line to point C.

Example 2-6. A simple path

```
100 100 m
100 200 l
200 200 l
```

If you were to use the S operator that you've seen in our examples so far, that would draw an L-shaped line, since it simply strokes the path as defined. However, if you used the s operator, you would instead have a triangle, since the path would be closed (i.e., connected from the last point back to the first point) and then stroked. You can explicitly close a path using the h operator as well, and then use S to stroke it—so you can therefore consider s as a nice shorthand.

Clipping

The final aspect of the model that we'll explore here is that of *clipping*. Clipping uses a path (or text) to restrict the drawing area from the full page to an arbitrary area on that page. This is most useful when you wish to show only a small portion of some other object (usually, but not necessarily limited to, raster graphics) for a specific visual effect.

Use the W operator to mark the path as a clipping path. You can then either continue to fill or stroke it (using the operators you've already seen), or do no drawing with the n operator.

Example 2-7. Rectangles clipped by a circle

```
q
    27.738 78.358 m
    27.738 56.318 45.604 38.452 67.643 38.452 c
    67.643 38.452 l
    89.681 38.452 107.548 56.318 107.548 78.358 c
    107.548 78.358 l
    107.548 100.396 89.681 118.262 67.643 118.262 c
    67.643 118.262 l
    45.604 118.262 27.738 100.396 27.738 78.358 c
    W n                     % clip with no actual drawing
    1 0 0 rg
    0 0 0 RG
    97.5 48.5 -98 97 re
    B
    0 0 1 rg
```

```
146.5 -0.5 -98 97 re
B
Q
```

Drawing Paths

While you could certainly do a lot of drawing with the three path construction operators you've seen so far (m, l, and re), you could do even more if you could draw something that wasn't straight—say a curve, for example.

The c operator allows you to draw a type of curve called a Bézier curve (Figure 2-1), and specifically a cubic Bézier. Such a curve is defined from the current point to a destination point, using two other points (known as *control points*) to define the shape of the curve. It requires a total of six operands.

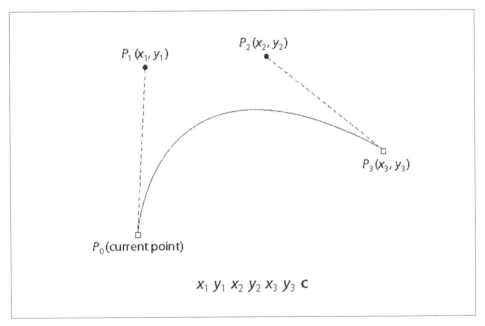

Figure 2-1. Example Bézier curve

While Bézier curves are extremely flexible and enable very complex drawings, they do have a fundamental flaw: they cannot be used to draw a perfect circle. The closest you can get is to combine four curves that start and end at the four edge points on the circle, using a control point about 0.6 units from the end points.

If you'd like to learn more about the mathematics for determining arcs and circles, the details can be found online.

Example 2-8 draws a circle, and also demonstrates how a path can be both stroked and filled using different colors.

Example 2-8. A dashed circle

```
1 0 0 rg
0 0 0.502 RG
2 w
[5 2 ] 0 d
350 200 m
350 227.6 327.6 250 300 250 c
272.4 250 250 227.6 250 200 c
250 172.4 272.4 150 300 150 c
327.6 150 350 172.4 350 200 c
B
```

Transformations

As discussed in the first chapter, each page (see "Pages" on page 26) defines an area (in user units) into which you can place content. Normally, the origin (0,0) of the page is at the bottom left of the page, with the *y* value increasing up the page and the *x* value increasing to the right. This is consistent with a standard Cartesian coordinate system's top-right portion. However, for certain types of drawing operations you may want to adjust (or *transform*, which is the proper term) the coordinates in some way—inverting/flipping, rotating, scaling, etc (see Figure 2-2).

The part of the graphic state that tracks this is called the *current transformation matrix* (CTM). To apply a transformation, you use the cm operator, which takes six operands that represent a standard 3x2 matrix. The chart below shows the most common types of transformations and which operands are used for them.

Transformation	Operand
Translation	1 0 0 1 tx ty

Scaling	sx 0 0 sy 0 0
Rotation	cosQ sinQ -sinQ cosQ 0 0
Skew	1 tanA tabB 1 0 0

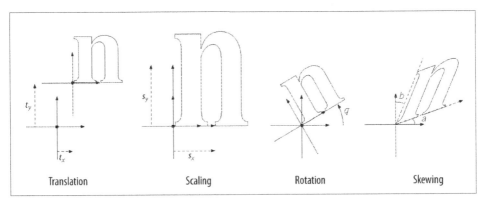

Figure 2-2. The four types of transformations

Example 2-9 gives a few examples of common transformations.

Example 2-9. Transformed shapes

```
q
    1 0 0 rg
    .50 0 0 .5 0 0 cm  % scale the drawing 50%
    0 0 100 100 re     % draw a 100x100 rect at the origin
    F
Q
q
    0 1 0 rg
    1 0 0 1 100 100 cm % move the origin to 100,100
    0 0 100 100 re     % draw a 100x100 rect at the origin
    F
Q
```

In some cases you will need to do multiple transformations, an operation called *concatenating the matrix.* The most common operation that requires concatenation is rotation (see Example 2-10). Not only is it more complex than other types of transformation since it involves the use of trigonometry, but it involves multiple operations. The reason for this in many cases is that rotation is always done around the bottom left of the object and not the center, which most people expect. Therefore, in order to handle rotation around the center point (or any arbitrary point), you need to first do a translation, and then a rotation, then transform back.

Example 2-10. A rotated rectangle

```
q
    0 1 0 rg
    1 0 0 1 50 50 cm                    % move origin to 50,50 (center point for
rect)
    0.7071 0.7071 -0.7071 0.7071 0 0 cm  % 45 deg rotation
    1 0 0 1 -50 -50 cm                   % move the origin back
    0 0 100 100 re                       % draw a 100x100 rect at the origin
    F
Q
```

Basic Color

In the examples so far, we've always used RGB-based colors (called DeviceRGB in PDF terms). That's the most common type of color that users are familiar with, since it's what computer monitors use. In each example, we've used either a 1 or a 0 for each individual color component value. Unlike in other RGB color systems, such as Windows GDI or HTML, in PDF the value for each component is a real number between 0 and 1 rather than an integer value between 0 and 255.

 If you need to convert, the math is quite simple: *pdfValue* = 255 − *gdiValue*/255.

PDF, however, supports ten other color spaces (or color models) that can be used to specify the color of an object. This section introduces the two other Device color spaces: DeviceGray and DeviceCMYK. To learn more about the other eight color spaces as well as how to use patterns or shading to stroke or fill an object, see ISO 32000-1:2008.

For colors that use only shades of black and white (or gray), you can use the simple *DeviceGray* color space. The operators are g (for fill) and G (for stroke), and they take a single operand ranging from 0 (black) to 1 (white). This color space should be used instead of RGB-based black whenever possible as it produces higher quality printing operations while saving space in the PDF (3 bytes per operation vs. 8 bytes per operation).

While screens use RGB to define colors, printers use a different model called CMYK, for the Cyan, Magenta, Yellow, and blacK ink cartridges that are present in the printer. Higher-end printers may also have various other color inks, but they are used in other ways. To describe a color in *DeviceCMYK*, you use the k or K operators along with four operands for each of the color components.

Example 2-11 illustrates the use of the three color spaces.

Example 2-11. The three basic color spaces

```
10 w
q
    .5 G        % 50% gray, in Gray
    10 300 m
    100 300 l
    S
Q
q
    1 0 0 RG    % red, in RGB
    10 200 m
    100 200 l
    S
Q
q
    1 0 0 0 K   % cyan, in CMYK
    10 100 m
    100 100 l
```

```
        S
Q
```

Marked Content Operators

In "Content Streams" on page 35, it was mentioned that there were a set of operators whose job was to simply mark a section of content for a specific purpose. These operators are called "marked content operators," and there are five of them, grouped into two categories. The MP and DP operators designate a single point in the content stream that is marked, while the BMC, BDC, and EMC operators bracket a sequence of content elements within the content stream.

 As stated, the marking *must* be around complete content elements and not simply a string of arbitrary bytes in the PDF. Additionally, the marked section *must* be contained within a single content stream.

To mark a single point in the content, perhaps to enable it to be easily located by a custom PDF processor, the MP or DP operator is used in conjunction with an operand of type Name, sometimes called a "tag." The difference between MP and DP is that the DP operator also takes a second operand, which is a property list (see "Property Lists" on page 47). Example 2-12 shows a few examples.

Example 2-12. Example of marked points

```
% a content stream somewhere in a PDF
% we are using ABCD_ as an arbitrary second class name
/ABCD_MyLine    MP
q
    10 10 m
    20 20 l
    S
Q

/ABCD_MyLineWithProps << /ABCD_Prop (Red Line) >> DP
q
    1 0 0 RG
    10 200 m
    100 200 l
    S
Q
```

In the same way, the BMC and BDC operators, respectively, take either just a single tag operand or the tag plus a property list. These operators, however, start a section of marked content whose end is defined by the EMC operator. As you can see in

Example 2-13, these operators are more useful than the simple point versions as they actually delineate the operators that are part of the group.

Example 2-13. Example of marked content

```
% a content stream somewhere in a PDF
% we are using ABCD_ as an arbitrary second class name
/ABCD_MyLine     BMC
    q
        10 10 m
        20 20 l
        S
    Q
EMC

/ABCD_MyLineWithProps << /ABCD_Prop (Red Line) >> BDC
    q
        1 0 0 RG
        10 200 m
        100 200 l
        S
    Q
EMC
```

Property Lists

When using the marked content operators DP and BDC, a dictionary is associated with the content as well. This dictionary is referred to as a *property list* and contains either information specific to the use of the content (such as with optional content) or private information meaningful to the writer creating the marked content (or a custom processor of the PDF).

Simple property lists, where all the values of all the keys are direct objects, may be written inline in the content stream as direct objects (as seen in the previous example). However, should any of the values of any of the keys require indirect references to objects outside the content stream, the property list dictionary needs to be defined as a named resource in the Properties subdictionary of the current resource dictionary and then referenced by name.

Resources

For content consisting only of paths in simple color spaces, the content stream is completely self-contained and needs no external references to other things. However, for most real-world PDF pages you will need other types of content, such as bitmap/raster images and text. These external references are managed via the resource dictionary that is the value of the Resources key in the page dictionary (see Example 2-14). Each key in the resource dictionary has a predefined name, based on the type of resource that is being listed. And the value of each key is itself a dictionary with the unique (and arbitrary) name for each resource and the indirect reference to the resource. It is common practice to use (short) identifying names/prefixes (such as GS for graphic state, IM for image, etc.) and then incrementally number as you go along. However, if you'd like to name them Manny, Moe, and Jack—that's fine too!

Example 2-14. Simple resources

```
% in the page dictionary
/Resources <<
    /Font <<
        /F1 10 0 obj
        /F2 11 0 obj
    >>
    /XObject <<
        /Im1 12 0 obj
    >>
>>
```

Don't worry too much about the details of resources yet; you'll be looking at them in specific examples as you continue.

External Graphic State

In all the examples we've looked at so far, all of the graphic state attributes have been applied directly in the content stream. This is mostly because we are using them only once, plus they happen to be simple attributes. However, there will be times when you'll want to keep something like a "predefined style" and simply reference it by name. Like stylesheets in other formats (such as HTML or DOCX), this allows for easy updating of the style without impacting the content (stream), while also keeping file size down and performance up. In PDF, these styles are invoked using something called a *graphic state parameter dictionary*, or *ExtGState* (short for External Graphic State, so called because they are external to the content stream).

To use one, you add the dictionary to the page dicitonary's resource dictionary (as an entry in the ExtGState dictionary, of course) and then use the gs operator in the content stream to invoke it. For example, to define a graphic state that uses a customized dash pattern at a large width, you could do the following (see Example 2-15):

Example 2-15. Using an ExtGState

```
% in the page dictionary
/Resources <<
    /ExtGState <<
        /GS0 <<
            /Type /ExtGState
            /LW 10                    % 10 wide
            /LC 1                     % rounded caps
```

```
          /D [[2 4 6 4 2] 2]          % dash pattern
      >>
    >>
>>

% in the content stream
/GS0 gs
0 1 0 0 K
100 100 m
100 400 l
S
```

Now that you've seen how to use ExtGStates as an alternative to inlining various attributes, let's look at something that can't be done inline, but only by using an ExtGState.

Basic Transparency

The PDF graphics model supports an extremely rich set of features in the area of transparency, which you can explore in detail in ISO 32000-1:2008, clause 11. For now, however, we'll look at some basic transparency that is similar to what you might be used to with other imaging models (such as GDI+).

The simplest type of transparency is applying a level or percentage (as a number from 0 to 1) to how transparent (or opaque) a given object is. An object with a transparency value of 0 is completely invisible, while a value of 1 (the default) is completely opaque. Any value in between means that whatever is underneath will show through (or, to use the technical term, will "blend" with the transparent object), to a greater or lesser extent. As with other graphic state attributes, you can set the stroke and fill transparency values separately using the CA and ca keys, respectively, in an ExtGState dictionary.

The reason that transparency is handled as part of the ExtGState dictionary instead of directly in the content stream was to provide compatibility with older readers at the time it was introduced into PDF (version 1.4). Example 2-16 gives a few exmaples of transparency.

Example 2-16. Three transparent rectangles

```
% in the page dictionary
/Resources <<
    /ExtGState <<
        /GS0 <<
            /CA 1
            /ca 1
        >>
        /GS1 <<
            /CA .5
            /ca .5
        >>
        /GS2 <<
            /CA .75
            /ca .75
        >>
    >>
>>

% in the content stream
q
    /GS0 gs     % no transparency
    1 0 0 rg
    209 426 -114 124 re
    f
Q
q
    /GS1 gs     % .5 transparency
    0 1 0 rg
    237 401 -114 124 re
    f
Q
q
    /GS2 gs     % .75 transparency
    0 0 1 rg
    272 373 -114 124 re
    f
Q
```

What's Next

In this chapter, you learned about content streams and many of the things that can be found inside them. You also learned about how to reference external things via named resources. However, so far we've only covered how to draw vector graphics (paths), not any of the other types of content that PDF supports—most especially, text and images.

Next we'll look at images, focusing on raster but also some additional ways to work with vector graphics. Following that, we'll tackle text.

CHAPTER 3

Images

In the previous chapter you learned how to create vector graphics, a series of lines and paths (and sometimes text) that have no predefined resolution and can be composed of multiple colorspaces and attributes. However, in many cases you may need to utilize a *raster image* (sometimes called a *bitmap image*) on your page. This chapter introduces them to you.

Raster Images

When most people think about raster images, they think about standard raster image formats such as JPEG, PNG, GIF, or TIFF. And while those formats do contain raster image data, they also contain all sorts of other things in a form of "image package." For PDF, however, you can't use the full package (except in one special case—see "JPEG Images" on page 54), and you need to "unwrap" it to get at the raw form that PDF expects.

This "raw form" is just a series of pixels, or in more technical terms, a two-dimensional array of those pixels (the two dimensions being the height of the image and the width of the image). For example, in Figure 3-1, the height is 40 pixels and the width is 46 pixels.

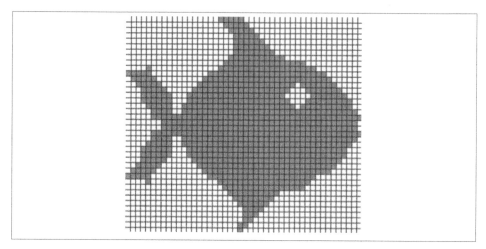

Figure 3-1. Large pixel (FatBits) image

Each of the pixels in that image, as mentioned previously, is really itself an array of values —one per number of colors (also known as *color components*) in the color space. If this were a *DeviceRGB* image, then each pixel would have three elements. However, if it were a *DeviceCMYK* image, there would be four, and if it were a *DeviceGray* image, there would be only one component. This shouldn't come as a surprise; it exactly matches the number of operands that the color space operators take! See "Basic Color" on page 44 for more on color space operators.

Finally, to understand how the data for the image is going to be arranged, you need to know how many bits of data are needed for each component of each pixel. Most developers only think in terms of 8 bits per component, which is why RGB images are sometimes referred to as 24-bit color images (8*3 = 24). But PDF supports a much richer set of options here, allowing 1, 2, 4, 8, or 16 bits per component (although in practice, only 1, 8, and 16 are used).

Adding the Image

To incorporate a raster image into a PDF and display it, you need to do three things:

1. Create an image dictionary and add the image data.
2. Add a reference to the image dictionary in a resource dictionary.
3. Refer to the resource in a content stream.

Image dictionaries

As with every other common PDF data structure, you need a dictionary to represent all the relevant information that you know about the image data. As you learned in "Stream

Objects" on page 7, image data itself lives in a stream, and thus the dictionary you are going to be working with will be in the stream's associated attributes dictionary.

The image dictionary is actually one type of *XObject* dictionary (XObject being short for eXternal Object, a graphic object that lives outside of or externally to the content stream). The other type will be the one you use for vector images. Because the objects are external, they can be referenced from multiple content streams without duplication.

 This is quite useful for graphics that appear on multiple pages of a document, such as company logos/letterheads or slide backgrounds.

Taking that as the basis for the dictionary, combined with all the attributes discussed earlier, we arrive at a dictionary that looks like the one in Example 3-1.

Example 3-1. Simple image dictionary

```
1 0 obj
<<
    /Type               /XObject
    /Subtype            /Image
    /Height             40
    /Width              46
    /ColorSpace         /DeviceRGB
    /BitsPerComponent   8
    /Length             5520    % 40*46*3
>>
stream
% pixel data goes here
endstream
endobj
```

Adding it to the resource dictionary is no different than the examples from the last chapter with ExtGState resources. So the resource dictionary would look something like Example 3-2.

Example 3-2. Image resource dictionary

```
% in the page dictionary
/Resources <<
    /XObject <<
        /Im1    1 0 R    % reference to our 1 0 obj in the previous example
    >>
>>
```

Images in content streams

The simple part of working with images in your content stream is knowing (and using) the Do operator, which takes a single operand: the name of the resource. However, if you only knew that and tried to just use it alone in the stream, like this:

```
/Im1 Do
```

you wouldn't see anything on the page and you'd wonder what went wrong.

What is wrong is that drawing image XObjects requires special handling of the CTM. If you want to understand the background for this, consult ISO 32000-1:2008, 8.9.4—but for now, the important thing to understand is that rather than the normal identity matrix of *1 0 0 1 0 0*, an image XObject has a default of *w 0 0 h 0 0* (where *w* is the image's width and *h* is its height in pixels, as defined in the image dictionary). Thus, for our image to appear in the lower-left corner of the page, without any scaling or other transforms, our content stream needs to look like Example 3-3.

Example 3-3. FatBits fish

```
q                % you don't need the q/Q, but it's a good habit!
46 0 0 40 0 0 cm
/Im1 Do
Q
```

As with the paths we worked with in the previous chapter, you can apply any combination of transformations to your image—scaling, rotation, etc. Just remember to always start with the image's size.

JPEG Images

One of the various filters that can be applied to a stream object is the DCTDecode filter. A *DCTDecode* stream is equivalent to a JFIF file, also known colloquially as a JPEG (or *.jpg/.jpeg*) file. JPEG files are the only standard image format that can be placed into a PDF without any modification—you just read the data stream from the file and then write it into the value of the stream object in the PDF, as shown in Example 3-4. Of course, you will either need to know a priori the size, colorspace, etc. of the image or have some way to parse the JPEG to obtain those values.

Example 3-4. PDF image based on JPEG data

```
1 0 obj
<<
        /Type            /XObject
        /Subtype         /Image
        /Height          246
        /Width           242
```

```
/ColorSpace          /DeviceRGB
/BitsPerComponent    8
/Length              16423
/Filter              /DCTDecode
>>
stream
% image data right from the JPEG goes here
endstream
endobj
```

Transparency and Images

While the normal behavior of an image in the PDF imaging model is for all of the pixels to be drawn on top of anything below them, there are ways that the image can express that some parts of itself are either completely or partially transparent. The original methods that PDF supports are called *masking*, as they completely "mask out" (off vs. on) a set of pixels based on the provided criteria. The newer methods use the same transparency model (see "Basic Transparency" on page 49) as that of paths, where you can have levels of transparency. Because we've already looked at that model, we'll cover that first.

Soft Masks

As you learned earlier, images in PDF are in a defined colorspace and as such have a defined number of components. In the case of RGB, there are three components: red, green, and blue. That means that there is no room for transparency information. The normal way to address this—as most common image formats, such as PNG and TIFF do—is to simply define a new color(space) with four components (ARGB or RGBA), where the fourth component of each pixel is its transparency value. However, as you also learned, one of the key goals when transparency was introduced in PDF was to maintain 100% backward compatibility with nontransparency-aware implementations. That prevented the use of a new colorspace.

So instead of the new colorspace, the transparency values for each pixel are stored in a separate image XObject. This "soft mask" image is referenced from the original image XObject via the SMask key in its dictionary. The soft mask image's dictionary is a standard image dictionary, subject to a few restrictions (see ISO 32000-1:2008, Table 145) —most importantly, the colorspace of the image must be *DeviceGray*. Allowing only *Device-Gray* makes perfect sense, since that's a one-component-per-pixel colorspace, which matches our missing component from RGBA/ARGB. This is also why in most cases the width and height of the parent image and its soft mask will match (although this is not required).

If you were to take the Example 3-3 from earlier and use a soft mask to make all the white parts transparent, you'd have something like Figure 3-2.

Figure 3-2. FatBits fish with a soft mask

```
% this is the soft mask
10 0 obj
<<
    /Type                /XObject
    /Subtype             /Image
    /BitsPerComponent    8
    /ColorSpace          /DeviceGray
    /Filter              /FlateDecode
    /Height              40
    /Width               46
    /Length              166    % smaller for compression
>>
stream
% masking data goes here
endstream
endobj

% this is the parent image
11 0 obj
<<
    /Type                /XObject
    /Subtype             /Image
    /BitsPerComponent    8
    /ColorSpace          /DeviceRGB
    /Filter              /FlateDecode
    /Height              40
    /Width               46
    /SMask               10 0 R
    /Length              166
>>
stream
% image data goes here
endstream
endobj
```

Stencil Masks

While soft masks are the most powerful, because they allow for varying levels of transparency, sometimes all you need is to be able to turn off a set of pixels so that they don't draw on top of whatever is behind them. The equivalent of a soft mask but with simple on/off properties is called a *stencil mask*. It works almost exactly like the soft mask, except that rather than the masked image being in *DeviceGray* at (usually) 8 bits per component, it has no colorspace and is always 1 bit per component. Each bit represents a pixel's on/off state, with 0 meaning on (mark) and 1 meaning off (leave alone). Should it be necessary, those values can be inverted through the presence of a Decode key in the stencil mask's image dictionary with a value of [1 0].

If you were to use a stencil mask to mask out the FatBits fish, it might look like Example 3-5.

Example 3-5. FatBits fish with a stencil mask

```
% this is the stencil mask
10 0 obj
<<
    /Type               /XObject
    /Subtype            /Image
    /ImageMask          true
    /BitsPerComponent   1
    /Height             40
    /Width              46
    /Length             230     % (40*46)/8
>>
stream
% masking data goes here
endstream
endobj

% this is the parent image
11 0 obj
<<
    /Type               /XObject
    /Subtype            /Image
    /BitsPerComponent   8
    /ColorSpace         /DeviceRGB
    /Filter             /FlateDecode
    /Height             40
    /Width              46
    /Mask               10 0 R
    /Length             166
>>
stream
% image data goes here
endstream
endobj
```

Color-Keyed Masks

In some cases, however, such as with our fish, all you really need to do is inform the PDF viewer that it should just ignore (mask) any pixels of a specific color (in our case, white). This simplest form of masking is called *color-key* (or *chroma-key*) *masking*, and it works like a blue screen in the movies. Anything that is in the defined color is not drawn.

To use a color-key mask in PDF, no secondary image is needed; you just need to know what color(s) you wish to have masked out. The Mask entry in the image dictionary will have as its value an array containing $2*n$ entries (where n is the number of components in the image's colorspace): each pair specifies the minimum and maximum values for that component to be masked. Therefore, for our RGB image, we need six values. Since we only want to mask out white, the minimum and maximum are both the same—255 (the value of white). Using this approach, the full image dictionary looks like Figure 3-3.

Figure 3-3. FatBits fish with a color mask

```
11 0 obj
<<
    /Type               /XObject
    /Subtype            /Image
    /BitsPerComponent   8
    /ColorSpace         /DeviceRGB
    /Filter             /FlateDecode
    /Height             40
    /Width              46
    /Mask               [255 255 255 255 255 255]
    /Length             166
>>
stream
% image data goes here
endstream
endobj
```

Vector Images

PDF doesn't really have the concept of a vector image, such as an EPS or EMF file. Instead, what it has is a way to encapsulate a content stream into a reusable object. As with raster images, this is another type of XObject called a *form XObject*.

 The name "form" here comes from the PostScript usage of the term; it has nothing to do with an *interactive form*, which is another type of PDF construct that you'll see in Chapter 7.

Adding the Form XObject

Just as with image XObjects, you need to do three things:

1. Create a form dictionary and add the data.

2. Add a reference to the form dictionary in a resource dictionary.

3. Refer to the resource in a content stream.

The Form Dictionary

A form XObject is a content stream (discussed in "Content Streams" on page 35) with a form dictionary associated with it that provides some extra intelligence and support to that content. Anything you can put in a page's content stream, you can put into a form XObject. This is very powerful since it enables a means to reuse an entire PDF page in some other context (for example, imposition or stamping). You'll see how to do that later in this chapter, but for now, let's take a look at the form dictionary's special fields.

There are four special keys in the form dictionary that are important in their creation:

BBox

> The most important one, and the only one that is required, is the BBox key. The BBox is an array representing a bounding box for the content. You can always use a rectangle larger than the actual content size, but a smaller one will cause your content to be clipped to that size.

Matrix

> The Matrix is a standard transformation matrix that will be applied to all instances of the XObject whenever it is drawn. It is almost always the identity matrix, since any specific transformation would be applied in the invoking content stream. Since the default value for the key is the identity, there is no reason to include this in the dictionary unless the transform is something else.

Resources

> Just like a page, your content stream may need extra resources (ExtGStates, fonts, etc.), and this is where you would reference them.

FormType

> This one is not only optional, but serves no practical purpose since there has only ever been a single value for it (1). Don't bother writing it into your PDFs; it only wastes space.

Example 3-6 shows a simple form XObject.

Example 3-6. Simple form XObject

```
1 0 obj
<<
    /Type           /XObject
    /Subtype        /Form
    /BBox           [0 0 100 100]
    /FormType       1  % optional, only here for example
```

```
    /Matrix            [1 0 0 1 0 0] % optional, only here for example
    /Length            180
>>
stream
    0 0 1 rg           % set the color to blue in RGB
    0 0 100 100 re     % draw a rectangle 100x100 with the bottom left at 0,0
    F                  % fill it
endstream
endobj
```

You would then add this to the page's resource dictionary and reference it in the content stream exactly as you did for the image (see Example 3-7). However, unlike with images, for form XObjects you use a standard CTM and don't need to worry about the size (since it's not described in pixels).

Example 3-7. Referencing the XObject in the page dictionary

```
% in the page dictionary
/Resources <<
    /XObject <<
        /Im1    1 0 R    % reference to our 1 0 obj in the previous example
    >>
>>


                       % in the page's content stream
q
        1 0 0 1 0 0 cm    % as with normal content, this means 100% at 0,0
    /Im1 Do
Q
```

The Do operator, when used with a form XObject, uses the keys we discussed earlier as part of its rendering or painting. The operations are as follows:

- Saves the current graphic state, as if by invoking the q operator
- Concatenates the matrix from the form dictionary's Matrix entry with the current transformation matrix (CTM)
- Clips according to the form dictionary's BBox entry
- Paints the graphics objects specified in the form's content stream
- Restores the saved graphic state, as if by invoking the Q operator

 Since the painting of the form XObject automatically invokes a q/Q pair, there is no need to have them as the start and end inside the form XObject's content stream.

Copying a Page to a Form XObject

If you are building a tool to impose or stamp PDF documents, one common operation is to convert a PDF page into a form XObject, so that it can easily be incorporated into any other page. Assuming you have a PDF library that is able to work with the object model of a PDF, the following instructions should help you do the conversion:

1. If the page has an array of content streams, combine them into a single one.

2. Compute the BBox based on the page's MediaBox and Rotate keys.

3. Copy the resource dictionary from the page to the form XObject (if you are doing this in the same PDF, use a shallow copy instead of a deep one).

 Since it is deprecated by ISO 32000-1:2008, you can remove the Proc Set key, if present.

What's Next

In this chapter, you learned about how PDF works with images—both raster and vector—via XObjects. Next, we'll look at drawing text.

CHAPTER 4

Text

In this chapter you will learn how to draw text on a page. Drawing text is the most complex part of PDF graphics, but it is also what helped PDF beat its competitors to become the international standard that it is today. While the other original players converted text to raster images or vector paths (to maintain the visual integrity), the inventors of PDF knew that users needed text that could be searched and copied and didn't just look pretty on the screen. With the depth of experience and understanding of fonts that Adobe's engineers had, they were able to integrate actual text with visual presentation.

While the text support in PDF enables the rendering of any glyphs from any font representing any language, the mechanics (as you'll see shortly) were all created prior to Unicode (*http://unicode.org/standard/WhatIsUnicode.html*). This means that many things that developers working in other file formats take for granted, such as just putting down Unicode codepoints and letting the renderer do all the hard work, have to be done manually with PDF.

Now that you've been given fair warning, let's start!

Fonts

In the previous chapters you learned how to draw vector graphics (or paths) as well as raster graphics (images) on a page. These types of drawing operations are fairly simple as they don't normally need extra information—it's just the instructions and (in the case of raster images) the image data. Text, however, requires more pieces. The most important of these pieces is the font.

Glyphs

A font, sometimes called a *font program*, is a collection of unique drawing instructions called *glyphs*. In general, each glyph is no different from the paths or rasters that you drew yourself in previous chapters. However, the font also contains a bunch of metadata about the various glyphs, including something called an *encoding* that provides a mapping from a known character set (such as ASCII, Unicode, or Shift-JIS) to the glyphs. Not every font has glyphs for every value in every encoding.

Figure 4-1 is an example of three common values in different encodings and their glyphs in different fonts.

	Arial	*Mistral*	Kozuka Mincho
ASCII 0x61	a	*a*	a
Unicode 0x03A6	Φ	□	Φ
Shift_JIS 0x8C91	□	□	倦

Figure 4-1. Example of glyphs in three different fonts

 The glyphs that look like rectangles are commonly known as "not-def" glyphs. Notdef (short for *not defined*) is a special glyph present in all fonts for the specific purpose of filling in when the requested glyph doesn't exist. If you see these in your PDFs, you know you did something wrong! (Though in this case, it's on purpose.)

While a glyph is primarily concerned with its shape and appearance, it also has a set of values associated with it called *glyph metrics*. These metrics, some of which are explicitly defined in the font itself while others are computed from a series of values, enable software to do such things as lay out text. For example, to draw "Hello" you need to know where to place the "e" after the "H." Figure 4-2 tells you to simply place the "e" at the "Next glyph origin."

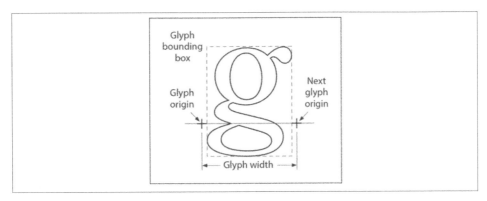

Figure 4-2. Various metrics shown around a glyph

Font Types

When graphical interfaces such as the original Lisa and Macintosh first came into existence, the fonts that came with them were known as "bitmapped fonts," because each glyph was described as a bitmap or raster image. While quite useful for the screen, this wasn't flexible enough for printing, so the outline (path-based) font formats were born. PDF supports the three most common outline formats:

Type 1
> This was the original outline format created by Adobe along with the Postscript language for printers. The glyph outlines are described using a simplified version of Postscript.

TrueType
> Created by Apple and Microsoft for their operating systems, this is the most well known of the font formats. Glyph outlines are described using a special language that is unique to this font format.

OpenType
> While Type 1 and TrueType fonts each have their advantages, the industry grew tired of the "font wars," so OpenType was born. OpenType combines the best of the other formats, with the option of glyph outlines being described either as Type 1 or as TrueType.

For these font types, the actual font program is defined in a separate font file, which may be either embedded in a PDF stream object or obtained from an external source.

PDF also has two types of fonts that are specific to PDF, where the glyph data must be defined in the PDF:

Type 3
> Originally provided as a way to embed bitmapped fonts, a Type 3 font is really a PDF dictionary where each glyph is defined by a standard content stream. This

allows not only raster-based glyphs, but the use of any/all PDF graphic operators to define the glyph. Although they can be very powerful, they are not used in most PDF-producing systems today.

Type 0

Also known as a composite font or CIDFont, a Type 0 font is created by taking glyph descriptions from one or more other fonts and creating an amalgam or composite. This was originally necessary when working with fonts in Chinese, Japanese, or Korean (CJK) that didn't also have English/Latin characters and a single font with both was desired. Though not used to actually amalgamate glyphs from multiple fonts, it is still the method used for Unicode fonts, especially when dealing with two-byte data.

The Font Dictionary

In Chapter 1, you saw our first PDF, which drew "Hello World" on the page. Example 4-1 shows a few relevant pieces that we're now going to look at in more detail.

Example 4-1. Parts of "Hello World.pdf"

```
1 0 obj
<<
    /Type /Page
    /Parent 5 0 R
    /MediaBox [ 0 0 612 792 ]
    /Resources 3 0 R
    /Contents 2 0 R
>>
endobj
3 0 obj
<<
    /Font <</F1 4 0 R >>
>>
endobj
4 0 obj
<<
    /Type /Font
    /Subtype /Type1
    /Name /F1
    /BaseFont/Helvetica
>>
endobj
```

In this example, you know that object #1 is the page, and it has just the bare minimum necessary: a MediaBox (for the size of the page), the Contents (for the drawing instructions), and the Resources (needed by the Contents). There is a single resource type, Font, with a single entry, F1, which is the font dictionary at object #4.

A font dictionary contains information that specifies the type of font (i.e., Type 1 or TrueType), its PostScript name, its encoding, and information that can be used to provide a substitute when the font program is not embedded in the PDF file.

ISO 32000-1:2008, 9.6.2.2 describes the Standard 14 (aka Base 14) fonts that every PDF renderer is required to know about and provide either directly or via appropriate substitutes. Additionally, the renderer is supposed to know about their metrics, which will enable us (for now) to not have to determine those values from the font program and incorporate them into the font dictionary. Object #4 in our example is quite small because it is using one of those fonts (Helvetica). The full list of standard fonts is:

- `Times-Roman`
- `Times-Bold`
- `Times-Italic`
- `Times-BoldItalic`
- `Helvetica`
- `Helvetica-Bold`
- `Helvetica-Oblique`
- `Helvetica-BoldOblique`
- `Courier`
- `Courier-Bold`
- `Courier-Oblique`
- `Courier-BoldOblique`
- `Symbol`
- `ZapfDingbats`

When creating a font dictionary for one of these fonts, there are only three required keys: `Type` (with a value of `Font`), `Subtype` (with a value of `Type1`), and `BaseName` (with one of the values from the preceding list).

You may have noticed that some of these fonts actually include what you might normally think of as a *style* (such as bold or italic). However, when working with PDF there are no styles, just fonts. So, if you want the Times font shown in italic, you need to use the font `Times-Italic`.

Example 4-2 is a variation of "Hello World" using a few different fonts.

Example 4-2. "Font World" (four different fonts)

Hello World

Hello World

Ηελλο Ωορλδ

Hello World

```
9 0 obj
<<
    /Type/Page
    /Contents 24 0 R
    /MediaBox[0 0 612 792]
    /Parent 5 0 R
    /Resources 13 0 R
>>
endobj
13 0 obj
<<
    /Font <<
        /F1 14 0 R
        /F2 13 0 R
        /F3 12 0 R
        /F4 11 0 R
    >>
>>
endobj
14 0 obj
<<
    /Type /Font
    /Subtype /Type1
    /BaseFont/Helvetica
>>
endobj
13 0 obj
<<
    /Type /Font
    /Subtype /Type1
    /BaseFont/Symbol
>>
endobj
12 0 obj
<<
    /Type /Font
    /Subtype /Type1
    /BaseFont/Courier-Bold
>>
endobj
11 0 obj
```

```
<<
    /Type /Font
    /Subtype /Type1
    /BaseFont/Times-Italic
>>
endobj
24 0 obj
<</Length 182>>
stream
BT
    /F1 48 Tf
    1 0 0 1 10 100 Tm
    (Hello World)Tj

    0 50 Td
    /F2 48 Tf
    (Hello World)Tj

    0 50 Td
    /F3 48 Tf
    (Hello World)Tj

    0 50 Td
    /F4 48 Tf
    (Hello World)Tj
ET
endstream
endobj
```

Encodings

The text that we've used so far has been simple English text. PDF, however, considers text associated with the Standard 14 fonts to be in something called *StandardEncoding*, which is a subset of ISO Latin-1 (ISO 8859-1) defined in ISO 32000-1:2008, D.2. If all the text in your PDFs can be expressed in that encoding, then you're good to go. However, most folks need at least the full Latin-1 to represent other standard characters used by other Roman/Latin-based languages such as French, Spanish, or German. To use those, you need to add an explicit encoding to the font dictionary, and continue to use simple text strings as you have done.

Here is an example of using *WinAnsiEncoding* (otherwise known as Windows code page 1252) to write out some text in other languages.

Example 4-3. Drawing text in other languages

Español
Français
English

```
14 0 obj
<<
    /Type /Font
    /Subtype /Type1
    /BaseFont/Helvetica
    /Encoding/WinAnsiEncoding
>>
endobj
24 0 obj
<</Length 182>>
stream
BT
    /F1 48 Tf
    1 0 0 1 10 100 Tm
    (English)Tj


    0 50 Td
    /F2 48 Tf
    (Français)Tj


    0 50 Td
    /F3 48 Tf
    (Español)Tj
ET
endstream
endobj
```

In order to support arbitrary non-Latin-based languages, it is necessary to use embedded fonts, a topic which is not covered in this edition of this book.

 It is possible to support Chinese, Japanese, and Korean (CJK) text in a PDF using nonembedded fonts, but it will require users who want to view the PDF to install extra fonts on their computers. We won't be covering how to do this, as it is not recommended.

Text State

Now that you have a good handle on fonts and glyphs, let's see how you can use them to actually draw text on the page (Example 4-4).

Example 4-4. Parts of Hello World.pdf

```
1 0 obj
<<
    /Type /Page
    /Parent 5 0 R
    /MediaBox [ 0 0 612 792 ]
    /Resources 3 0 R
    /Contents 2 0 R
>>
endobj
2 0 obj
<< /Length 53 >>
stream
BT
    /F1 24 Tf
    1 0 0 1 260 600 Tm
    (Hello World)Tj
ET
endstream
endobj
```

If you examine the content stream at object #2, you will see five new operators that you haven't seen before. The first one, BT, appears all by itself (i.e., with no operands) on the first line. As you can probably guess, it is stands for "Begin Text" and is required to delineate a series of text-related instructions. It is paired with the ET (End Text) operator, which can be seen on the last line of the content stream.

Just as PDF has a graphic state (see "Graphic State" on page 36 for more on this), it also has a text state that incorporates all the text–drawing-related attributes. The BT/ET pairing declares a new text state and then clears it, much as q and Q do with the graphic state. However, there is no push/pop. In fact, it is not permitted to have nested pairs of BT/ET.

Font and Size

While there are many attributes in a text state, and you'll look at a few here, the three most important are the font to be used, the text size, and where to put the text.

The Tf operator specifies the name of a font resource—that is, an entry in the font subdictionary of the current resource dictionary. The value of that entry is a font dictionary (see "The Font Dictionary" on page 66). In the previous example, the font is named F1, and if you refer back to Figure 4-1 you can see that it is present in the Font resources in object #3.

As you learned in "Transformations" on page 42, PDF uses a general "user unit" concept for defining the size and location of objects. In PDF, the standard glyph size is 1 unit in user space, and the nominal height of tightly spaced lines of text is also 1 unit. Therefore, in order to draw a glyph at a specific size, you need to scale it. The scale factor is specified as the second operand of the Tf operator, thereby setting the text font size parameter in the graphic state. In our example, the font size is 24.

There is a second way to set the scale factor for the glyphs, which is similar to how other graphic objects are scaled—using a transformation matrix. For text-specific transformations, you use the Tm operator, which takes the same parameters as the cm operator we looked at in Chapter 2. In our example, no additional scaling is taking place but the text is being positioned at (260,600). This is the normal way of setting the scaling and position for your first glyph to be drawn. However, it could also be done this way:

```
/F1 1 Tf
24 0 0 24 260 600 Tm
(Hello World)Tj
```

Is one way better than the other? On modern systems and current implementations, the differences should be indistinguishable. If you are trying for the best possible implementation of your content, it will depend on how the font is used. If you are only using the text at a single size (on a given page), using the scale factor as part of the Tf is best, because then the glyphs will be prescaled by the font loader. However, should you be using the same font at multiple sizes on the page, then loading at 1 unit and using Tm to scale each time is probably more optimal—but only if you are switching back and forth a lot. Otherwise, just create a second instance of the font with a second Tf, as shown in Example 4-5.

Example 4-5. Drawing in both big and little text

Big Text

Small Text

```
BT
    /F1 24 Tf
    1 0 0 1 100 150 Tm
    (Big Text)Tj

    /F1 12 Tf
    1 0 0 1 100 100 Tm
    (Small Text)Tj
ET
```

Rendering Mode

In "The Painter's Model" on page 39, you learned that paths drawn in PDF can be filled, stroked, or both, based on the operator (e.g., f vs. S) that ends the path description. With text, instead of using different operators, there is a single operator (Tr) that sets the text rendering mode. Figure 4-3 lists the possible operand values that can be used with Tr and the impact they have on the text.

	Rendering mode	Description
R	0	Fill text
R	1	Stroke text
R	2	Fill then stroke text
	3	Text with no fill and no stroke (invisible)
R	4	Fill text and add it to the clipping path
R	5	Stroke text and add it to the clipping path
R	6	Fill then stroke text and add it to the clipping path
R	7	Add text to the clipping path

Figure 4-3. The seven text rendering modes

When you combine the rendering modes with the graphic state attributes that you already know about, you can create the text in Example 4-6.

Example 4-6. Stroked and filled text

```
BT
    /F1 80 Tf
    1 0 0 1 100 100 Tm
    1 0 0 RG
    [2] 0 d
    0.75 g
    2 Tr
    (ABC)Tj
ET
```

Drawing Text

In case you hadn't figured it out by now, the Tj operator is used to draw text (also known as "showing" a string) on a page. It is quite simple, in that the operator causes the PDF renderer to align the first glyph's "glyph origin" with the current pen location and draw the glyph. Then the renderer advances the pen by the width of the glyph to the "next glyph origin" and draws the next glyph, and so on for the entire string.

For the majority of text rendering, this is perfectly acceptable and what most users are used to seeing on the screen. However, for those instances where you wish more precise control over glyph positioning, you will need to use the TJ operator.

Many fonts include information about how to more precisely place certain glyphs in relation to each other, known as *kerning*. However, this is not supported by the Tj operator when drawing a string. If you want to use that information, you need to obtain it from the font yourself and then use the TJ operator to obtain the more visually appealing result.

The TJ operator, instead of taking a string as an operand, takes an array. The array consists of one or more strings interspersed with numbers, where the numbers serve to adjust the text position (Tm). The numbers are expressed in thousandths of a unit, and the value is subtracted from the current horizontal coordinate.

This means that in the default coordinate system, a positive adjustment has the effect of moving the next glyph painted to the left by the given amount, while a negative adjustment will move the next glyph to the right.

Example 4-7 shows drawing a word using the simple Tj operator, and manually kerning it via TJ.

Example 4-7. Manually kerned text

```
BT
 /F1 48 Tf
 1 0 0 1 10 150 Tm
(AWAY)Tj
 1 0 0 1 10 100 Tm
[ (A) 120 (W) 120 (A) 95 (Y) ] TJ
ET
```

Positioning Text

In all of the previous examples, the text has been explicitly positioned using the Tm operator. However, that is a fairly heavyweight operation if all you want to do is move the pen in a single direction (e.g., down to the next line, or over to the right). For simpler movements, the Td operator should be used. It takes two parameters, t_x and t_y, representing how to move the pen in the X and Y directions (respectively). If either parameter is 0, the pen isn't moved in that direction. Example 4-8 illustrates using Td to draw a "4-square."

Example 4-8. A "4 square" of numbers

```
BT
    /F1 48 Tf
    1 0 0 1 10 700 Tm
    (1)Tj
    0 -50 Td
    (2)Tj
    50 50 Td
    (3)Tj
    0 -50 Td
    (4)Tj
ET
```

Remember that in PDF, the *y* coordinate is 0 at the bottom of the page, so to draw text down the page, you start high and subtract.

What's Next

In this chapter, you learned about fonts and glyphs and how to use them to draw text. Next you'll move from putting content on a page to making your document more interactive with navigational features.

CHAPTER 5

Navigation

Although you've spent the last three chapters talking strictly about static content, there is much more to PDF. This chapter will introduce various ways in which a PDF can gain interactivity, specifically around enabling navigation within and between documents.

Destinations

A *destination* defines a particular view of a document. It will always refer to a specific page of the PDF, and may optionally include a smaller subsection of the page as well as a magnification (zoom) factor.

Destinations don't stand alone; they are the values of keys in specific dictionaries related to parts of a PDF that could cause the invocation of an associated action. For example, in the document catalog, a destination can be the value of the `OpenAction` key. When present, that instructs the viewer to jump to that destination immediately upon opening the document.

 A common use of `OpenAction` is to jump to the first page of actual document content, which may come after some preface material that most users will not be interested in reading.

Explicit Destinations

Since the number of things that make up a destination is small and well defined, a destination is not based on a dictionary but instead on an array, unlike the other types of common objects that you've encountered so far (see Example 5-1). The first element of the array is always an indirect reference to the page object to which it refers, followed by a name object describing the type of zoom, and then any additional options needed for that zoom.

Example 5-1. Examples of destinations

```
% Object 1 is assumed to be the page

[1 0 R /Fit]          % Display entire page with horizontal & vertical magnified to
fit

[1 0 R /FitH]         % Display entire page with only horizontal magnified to fit
[1 0 R /FitH 100]     % FitH variant where vertical top is 100

[1 0 R /FitV]         % Display entire page with only vertical magnified to fit
[1 0 R /FitV 100]     % FitH variant where horizontal left is 100
```

In addition to Fit, FitH, and FitV, there are other ways to zoom into a specific part of a page; the most powerful of these is XYZ, which includes the specific left and top coordinates of the page (for the viewer to align with) along with the zoom factor. If you don't know them or want any of the top, left, or zoom factor values to change from what they are when the destination is invoked, provide a 0 or null value. Example 5-2 illustrates the use of XYZ.

Example 5-2. Examples of destinations

```
% Object 1 is assumed to be the page

[1 0 R /XYZ 36 36 50]    % Display a portion of the page, 1/2 inch in from the top
and left and zoomed 50%

[1 0 R /XYZ null null 50] % Display the current portion of the page, zoomed 50%
```

Named Destinations

Instead of being defined directly using the syntax shown previously, a destination may be referred to indirectly by means of a string.

This capability is especially useful when the destination is located in another PDF document. For example, a document (DocA) that wished to link to the beginning of Chapter 2 in another document (DocB) could refer to that destination by a name (e.g., *Chapter2*), instead of by an explicit page number in the other document. This would enable the actual physical page number of that chapter in DocB to change (due to edits, page insertions/deletions, etc.) without invalidating the destination in DocA.

Named destinations work by creating a correspondence between the name (which is represented as a string object) and the destination. This correspondence or mapping happens via the document's name dictionary, which is the value of the Names key in the document's catalog dictionary. In the name dictionary is a Dests key, whose value is a name tree with the string → destination mapping.

A name tree is similar to a dictionary in that it enables associating a key with a value; however, rather than using a name object as the key it uses a string object and it requires that the strings be sorted.

The destination value associated with a key in the name tree may be either an array or a dictionary. When the value of this entry is a dictionary, each key is a destination name and the corresponding value is either an explicit destination or a dictionary with a D entry whose value is an explicit destination.

Actions

Although destinations can be used by themselves, sometimes you need to incorporate them into an action in order for them to be usable. An *action*, as the name implies, is a form of command that is present in the document that invokes a particular behavior (action) in the viewer. There are both implicit actions and explicit actions. An *implicit action* happens through normal document navigation, such as the OpenAction that is invoked when a document is first opened, while an *explicit action* happens when the user interacts with some other object in the PDF, such as a button (see "Button Fields" on page 109) or bookmark (see "Bookmarks or Outlines" on page 83).

The Action Dictionary

The action dictionary is the common base dictionary for all types of actions. It consists of only one required entry: the S key, whose value declares the type of action. All other keys in this dictionary will vary based on the type of action.

GoTo Actions

The most common action is GoTo. The GoTo action corresponds to a destination, in that its invocation will cause a viewer to "go to" a specific destination. This is clear when you see that the main key in the GoTo action dictionary is the D key, whose value is a destination. See Example 5-3.

Example 5-3. Simple GoTo link

```
% This is the action dictionary for a GoTo action
8 0 obj
<<
    /Type /Action
    /S /GoTo
    /D [10 0 R /Fit] % GoTo the page referred by object 10 and fit it
>>
endobj

% This is an object called a link annotation
```

```
9 0 obj
<<
    /Type /Annot
    /Subtype /Link
    /Rect [100 100 150 150]
    /A 8 0 R
>>
endobj
```

In this example, object #8 represents a GoTo action that will take the user to a page in the document (referenced by object #10) and display it as magnified to Fit (as per the explicit destination that is the value of the D key). However, this action can't stand by itself—it needs to be connected to some other object that will cause it to be invoked by the viewer implicitly, or the user explicitly. In this example, it is connected to an object (#9) called a *link annotation*.

 A link annotation is an object that provides a clickable area on the page associated with an action. You'll learn more about annotations in Chapter 6.

URI Actions

The second most common action is URI. A URI (uniform resource identifier) is a more flexible concept than the normal URL (uniform resource locator) that most users are familiar with, though for the vast majority of cases you can use them interchangeably. So you can just think of the URI action as a web link.

Like the GoTo action, a URI action is very simple; it involves the addition of a single key (URI) to the standard action dictionary (see Example 5-4).

Example 5-4. Simple URI link

```
% This is the action dictionary for a URI action
8 0 obj
<<
    /Type /Action
    /S /URI
    /URI (http://www.oreilly.com)
>>
endobj

9 0 obj
<<
    /Type /Annot
    /Subtype /Link
    /Rect [100 100 150 150]
    /A 8 0 R
```

```
>>
endobj
```

The value of the URI key can be any valid URI. It is not limited to common schemes such as *http* or *ftp*; it could use a historical scheme such as *gopher* or a custom or private scheme such as *book*. The reason is that a PDF reader is not required to support any specific schemes and will usually just pass the URI off to the operating system for processing.

GoToR and Launch Actions

You've seen how GoTo actions can be quite useful, as long as you only need to navigate inside of the same PDF document. Similarly, the URI action enables redirecting the user to documents and web pages that are online. However, sometimes you want to refer to something in another PDF, or even another type of document (e.g., a word processing document or spreadsheet). For those situations you will need to use either a GoToR (for PDF) or a Launch (for other file types) action.

The GoToR action, also known as the "remote go-to" action, incorporates all of the aspects of a GoTo action, but with the addition of an F key in the action dictionary that points to the PDF in which the destination is to be resolved. A common use for this would be in a book that is broken up into chapters, where you want links between the chapters. Example 5-5 illustrates how to use GoToR to open up a PDF called "Chapter2.pdf" (which is in the same directory as the link's PDF) and go to physical page #1.

Example 5-5. Example of a GoToR action

```
% This is the action dictionary for a GoTo action
8 0 obj
<<
    /Type /Action
    /S /GoToR
    /D [0 /Fit] % NOTE: GoToR uses zero-based page #s, not indirect references
    /F <<
        /Type /Filespec
        /F (Chapter2.pdf)
        /UF (Chapter2.pdf)
    >>
endobj
```

 You may wonder why you have the same string (Chapter2.pdf) as values for both the F and UF keys in the GoToR action dictionary. The reason is that UF is preferred in modern PDF readers, since the value there could be a Unicode string, while F is there for historical reasons. So, to ensure the best results, you always write both.

For those situations where you need to externally link to a non-PDF document, the Launch action provides the solution. As you can see in Example 5-6, its syntax is almost exactly the same as that of the GoToR action.

Example 5-6. Example of a Launch action

```
% This is the action dictionary for a Launch action
8 0 obj
<<
    /Type /Action
    /S /Launch
    /F <<
        /Type /Filespec
        /F (Chapter2.docx)
        /UF (Chapter2.docx)
    >>
>>
endobj
```

Multimedia Actions

We've only touched the surface of actions with the four types of actions covered so far. There are also actions that enable the PDF to play sounds and movies, work with embedded 3D objects, and even run a JavaScript program. We'll discuss these in Chapter 9; see also ISO 32000-1:2008, 12.6.

Nested Actions

One of the other advantages of using an action over a simple destination is that you can combine multiple actions, using the Next key in the action dictionary to chain them together. For example, the effect of clicking a link annotation with the mouse might be to play a sound, jump to a new page, and start up a movie.

The Next entry is not restricted to a single action but may contain an array of actions, each of which in turn may have a Next entry of its own. The actions therefore form a tree instead of a simple linked list. Actions within each Next array are executed in order, each followed in turn by any actions specified in its Next entry, and so on recursively.

> Actions, including their Next values, are always processed in a depth-first traversal to ensure that their order of processing is consistent. This also provides you with insurance that the document state will be what you expect as each action is processed.

Bookmarks or Outlines

It's very common for structured documents to contain a tree-structured hierarchy of outline items that the reader presents to the user. These outline items allow the user to navigate interactively from one part of the document to another via their presentation as a visual table of contents separate from the actual page content. When such an item is activated, such as by the user clicking the text of an outline item in his UI, the conforming reader navigates to the destination or invokes the action associated with the item.

 Unlike some other book or reading formats, PDF combines author-controlled navigation entries (such as "Table of Contents" and "Chapter 1") with user-added links (bookmarks) to their favorite sections.

The root of a document's outline hierarchy is an outline dictionary specified by the Outlines entry in the document catalog (see "The Catalog Dictionary" on page 21). Each individual outline item within the hierarchy is defined by an outline item dictionary. The items at each level of the hierarchy form a doubly linked list, chained together through their Prev and Next entries and accessed through the First and Last entries in the parent item (or in the outline dictionary in the case of top-level items). When displayed on the screen, the items at a given level appear in the order in which they occur in the linked list.

In a large or complex document, the outline hierarchy may be very large and deep, and having it displayed in its entirety by the viewer would be counter-productive. To this end, each outline item that has children can also specify if the children are to be displayed (open) or hidden (closed). Unfortunately, the key that is used to specify the visibility is also the key that is used for the number of outline entries—Count.

Count is defined as the "sum of the number of visible descendent outline items at all levels." However, sometimes the value is negative. How can it be a sum if it's negative? The sign of the sum represents whether the outline item is to be displayed open or closed in the reader's UI. If the number is positive, then the children are shown; if negative, then the children are hidden.

In Example 5-7, you can see that there will be five visible outline items shown by the reader, since the Count in object 21 is positive. However, as you can see in the following figure, not all of those five are top-level items (direct children of the root)—there are only two of those (objects 22 and 29). You can see that these are the root's children by following the First link from objects 21 to 22, then the Next link from objects 22 to 29. Object 22 has three children (which will all be visible): objects 25, 26, and 28. And finally, object 26 has a single child (object 27), but it will be shown as closed because the value of Count for this object is –1.

Example 5-7. Sample outline

On-screen appearance	Object number	Count
Document	21	5
	22	3
Section 1	25	0
Section 2	26	-1
Section 3	28	0
Summary	29	0

```
21 0 obj
<<
    /Type /Outlines
    /First 22 0 R
    /Last 29 0 R
    /Count 5
>>
endobj
22 0 obj
<<
    /Title (Document)
    /Parent 21 0 R
    /Next 29 0 R
    /First 25 0 R
    /Last 28 0 R
    /Count 3
    /Dest [3 0 R /XYZ 0 792 0]
>>
endobj
25 0 obj
<<
    /Title (Section 1)
    /Parent 22 0 R
    /Next 26 0 R
    /Dest [3 0 R /XYZ null 701 null]
>>
endobj
26 0 obj
<<
    /Title (Section 2)
    /Parent 22 0 R
    /Prev 25 0 R
    /Next 28 0 R
    /First 27 0 R
    /Last 27 0 R
    /Count -1
    /Dest [3 0 R /XYZ null 680 null]
>>
endobj
```

```
27 0 obj
<<
    /Title (Subsection 1)
    /Parent 26 0 R
    /Dest [3 0 R /XYZ null 670 null]
>>
endobj
28 0 obj
<<
    /Title (Section 3)
    /Parent 22 0 R
    /Prev 26 0 R
    /Dest [7 0 R /XYZ null 500 null]
>>
endobj
29 0 obj
<<
    /Title (Summary)
    /Parent 21 0 R
    /Prev 22 0 R
    /Dest [8 0 R /XYZ null 199 null]
>>
endobj
```

The preceding example is the most common type of document outline, where all of the items use destinations to point to specific parts of the document. However, instead of a Dest key, any outline item can have an A key pointing to an action.

For instance, as shown in Example 5-8, you could have an outline item that uses a URI action to take the user to an online game associated with the document.

Example 5-8. An outline with a URI action

```
29 0 obj
<<
    /Title (Play Online Game)
    /Parent 21 0 R
    /Prev 22 0 R
    /A <<
        /Type /Action
        /S /URI
        /URI (http://www.someexamplegamesite.com)
    >>
>>
endobj
```

What's Next

In this chapter you learned about various types of navigational features that can be added to a PDF, including bookmarks and actions. In the next chapter, we will dive deeper into annotations.

CHAPTER 6

Annotations

This chapter will go into detail on a special type of object in PDF—the annotation. Annotations are PDF objects that enable user-clickable actions as well as new types of content including 3D, video, and audio.

Introduction

The content that a user sees on a PDF page is described using a content stream of PDF graphic operators (see "Content Streams" on page 35 for more). However, sometimes it is necessary to overlay that content with active or "hot" areas, or additional graphics. You may also want to incorporate new types of content onto your pages, such as 3D graphics or videos that cannot be described using those graphic operators. To accomplish these things, the annotation object is used.

As with page content, annotations are associated directly with a page. In any page dictionary for a page containing annotations, there has to be an `Annots` key whose value is an array of the annotations.

Annotation Dictionaries

Annotation objects are dictionary objects containing at least two keys: `Rect` and `Subtype`. The `Rect` key, of course, has a value that is a rectangle representing the page coordinates where the annotation is to be placed by the viewing application. The `Subtype` key has a name value that represents which one of the 27 types of annotations is being described by this particular dictionary. Many types of annotations will also have a `Contents` key whose value is a text string that is displayed either directly on the page or is an alternate description of the annotation's content in a human-readable form. Depending on the type of annotation, the other keys in the annotation dictionary may be either required or optional. Some of these keys are common to all types of annotations, while others are specific to a particular type.

ISO 32000 separates annotations into two categories: markup (discussed below) and non-markup (discussed in "Non-Markup Annotations" on page 102). ISO 32000-1 defines most annotations as being markup annotations because they are used primarily to mark up the content of a PDF document. Additionally, these annotations have text that appears as part of the annotation and may be displayed in other ways by a conforming reader.

Appearance Streams

Annotation dictionaries may contain entries that describe shapes and colors to be drawn by the PDF viewer, instead of a content stream. However, a PDF that requires a guaranteed appearance may also associate a special type of content stream, called an *appearance stream*, with an annotation. It does this by including an AP key in the annotation dictionary whose value is an appearance dictionary that references one or more appearance streams. When an appearance stream is present, the viewer will simply draw that instead of recreating the drawing instructions using the other values.

The appearance dictionary that references the appearance stream can have up to three keys present: N (the normal appearance), R (the rollover appearance), and D (the down appearance). For the types of annotations discussed here, we only use the N key, but AcroForms, discussed in Chapter 7, supports the others.

An example of using an appearance stream can be found in Figure 6-6.

Markup Annotations

As the name implies, these types of annotations are used to apply various types of common markup operations on top of the page content. There are many types of markups that can be applied (shown in Table 6-1), from the simple *Highlight* and *StrikeOut* to the generic *Ink*, and the specialized *Redact*.

Table 6-1. Markup annotations

Annotation type	Description
Caret	Caret annotation
Circle	Circle annotation
FileAttachment	File attachment annotation
FreeText	Free text annotation
Highlight	Highlight annotation
Ink	Ink annotation
Line	Line annotation
Polygon	Polygon annotation
PolyLine	Polyline annotation

Annotation type	Description
Redact	Redact annotation
Square	Square annotation
Squiggly	Squiggly-underline annotation
Sound	Sound annotation
Stamp	Rubber stamp annotation
StrikeOut	Strikeout annotation
Text	Text annotation
Underline	Underline annotation

Text Markup

These are the types of annotations that most users are familiar with when commenting on a PDF—highlight, underline, and strike out, along with the unusual addition of the squiggly (a jagged underline).

In each case, the `Subtype` will be one of those four values (`Highlight`, `Underline`, `StrikeOut`, or `Squiggly`) and the `Rect` will encompass the area on the page (usually covering text) in which the graphical representation of the annotation will be drawn. Additionally, we want to define the color that the annotation will be drawn in, so the `C` key will be used.

The value of the `C` key is an array of either 1, 3, or 4 values representing not only the color value but also (implicitly) the color space in which that value should be handled. A one-element array represents DeviceGray, three elements for DeviceRGB and four elements for DeviceCMYK. Figure 6-1 shows a few sample text markup annotations.

Figure 6-1. Text markup annotations

```
9 0 obj
<<
    /Type       /Page
    /Annots     [ 20 0 R  22 0 R  24 0 R  26 0 R ]
    % other stuff that we need for a valid page dictionary
```

```
    >>


20 0 obj
<<
    /Type          /Annot
    /Subtype       /Highlight
    /Rect          [ 252.594 593.733 322.077 623.211 ]
    /C             [ 1 1 0 ]
    >>


22 0 obj
<<
    /Type          /Annot
    /Subtype       /StrikeOut
    /Rect          [ 313.07 592.866 392.279 624.078 ]
    /C             [ 1 0 0 ]
    >>


24 0 obj
<<
    /Type          /Annot
    /Subtype       /Underline
    /Rect          [ 251.727 528.21 322.944 559.422 ]
    /C             [ 0 1 0 ]
    >>


26 0 obj
<<
    /Type          /Annot
    /Subtype       /Squiggly
    /Rect          [ 313.07 528.21 392.279 559.422 ]
    /C             [ 0 0 1 ]
    >>
```

If the text being annotated is rotated or otherwise transformed, you can use the Quad
Points key to define an array of eight points representing the four corners of a quad-
rilateral that bounds the text.

Although you don't need QuadPoints for simple rotations (0, 90, 180,
270), it won't hurt to have one since a rect described in eight points
instead of four is perfectly acceptable.

Figure 6-2 shows an example of highlighted text that is also being rotated.

Figure 6-2. Rotated highlighting

```
51 0 obj
<<
    /Type         /Annot
    /Subtype      /Highlight
    /Rect         [ 258.483 291.978 368.238 401.733 ]
     /QuadPoints   [ 259.709 312.822 347.394 400.507 279.327 293.204 367.012
380.889 ]
    /C            [ 1 1 0 ]
>>
```

Even though a QuadPoints array is more specific than the Rect, the Rect is always required to be present because it serves as a "maximum bounding area" for the QuadPoints. In fact, ISO 32000-1 says "QuadPoints shall be ignored if any coordinate in the array lies outside the region specified by Rect."

Drawing Markup

PDF defines a series of six types of annotations that enable drawing-like operations that can be used to mark up a PDF. While it is unfortunate that each of them has a slightly different way of describing the graphic shape that is being represented, they all support a standard set of attributes such as colors, weights, and more.

Attributes

The two most common attributes describe the lines (or strokes, if you prefer) that are being drawn: the color (and associated color space) as well as the line weight and any dash pattern. Both the C (stroke) and the IC (fill) keys use an array of numbers to specify the color space and the color values, as described earlier in "Text Markup" on page 89.

The BS key has a border style dictionary as its value. As described in ISO 32000-1:2008, Table 166, this dictionary consists of only two possible keys: S for the border style and D for a dash array. The border style can have values that specify a solid border (S), a dashed border (D), different types of embossing (B and I), and an underline style (U). The dash array takes the same form as it does when including it in a content stream.

The embossing styles are primarily useful for shapes. Although you can specify them on a simple line, you will probably not obtain the effect you desire.

Squares and circles

The square and circle annotations are the simplest of the drawing annotations, in that they don't need any extra keys in their dictionaries. Instead, they rely on the existing Rect key for the shape bounding area and the BS and IC keys for any styling.

 For square and circle annotations, the value of the IC key is used to fill the entire shape, much as the F operator would fill a shape in a content stream.

One nice additional key that can be specified on these annotations is the BE key, which can be used to turn a simple circle (or rectangle) into one that resembles a cloud. The BE key's value is a border effect dictionary that can contain either an S key (with a value of S for "simple" or a C for "cloudy") or an I key with an integer value between 0 and 2 that declares the intensity of the effect.

When including a border effect (BE), it is frequently useful to include an RD key in the annotation dictionary. It allows for the specification of an "offset margin" from the bounding rectangle to the one used to draw the shape. Figure 6-3 shows a few examples of square and circle annotations.

Figure 6-3. Examples of square and circle annotations

```
% A red stroked square
60 0 obj
<<
    /C [ 1 0 0 ]
    /RD [ 0.50 0.50 0.50 0.50 ]
    /Rect [ 281.239990 680.687012 355.390991 754.838013 ]
    /Subtype Square
    /Type Annot
>>
```

```
% A circle stroked in (RGB) green and filled in (grayscale) gray
62 0 obj
<<
    /BS << /W 3 >>
    /C [ 0 1 0 ]
    /IC [ .50 ]
    /RD [ 1.50 1.50 1.50 1.50 ]
    /Rect [ 375.842987 680.411011 456.338989 760.908020 ]
    /Subtype Circle
    /Type Annot
>>

% A blue circle with a cloud effect
64 0 obj
<<
    /BE << /I 2 /S C >>
    /BS << /W 2 >>
    /C [ 0 0 1 ]
    /RD [ 1 1 1 1 ]
    /Rect [ 483.533997 685.257019 551.442993 753.164978 ]
    /Subtype Circle
    /Type Annot
>>
```

Lines

The *line* annotation is used to draw a simple line. It has a single required key in its dictionary: L, which is an array of four numbers that specify the two endpoints of the line.

One additional key that the line annotation dictionary supports is the LE key, which allows the specification of different types of line endings, including arrowheads, boxes, and circles (see Figure 6-4). There are 10 different types of possible line endings, as you can see in Table 6-2.

Table 6-2. Types of line endings for line annotations

Name	Description
Square	A square filled with the annotation's interior color, if any
Circle	A circle filled with the annotation's interior color, if any
Diamond	A diamond shape filled with the annotation's interior color, if any
OpenArrow	Two short lines meeting in an acute angle to form an open arrowhead
ClosedArrow	Two short lines meeting in an acute angle, as in the OpenArrow style, and connected by a third line to form a triangular closed arrowhead filled with the annotation's interior color, if any
None	No line ending
Butt	A short line at the endpoint perpendicular to the line itself
ROpenArrow	Two short lines angled in the reverse direction from OpenArrow

Name	Description
RClosedArrow	A triangular closed arrowhead in the reverse direction from ClosedArrow
Slash	A short line at the endpoint approximately 30 degrees clockwise from perpendicular to the line itself

 For line annotations, the value of the IC key is used to fill only the line ending.

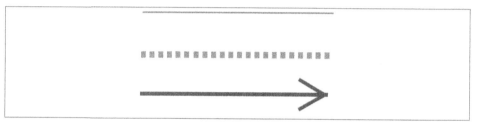

Figure 6-4. Examples of line annotations

```
% Simple red line
20 0 obj
<<
    /Type Annot
    /Subtype Line
    /C [ 1 0 0 ]
    /L [ 30.098700 755.213013 204.001999 755.213013 ]
    /Rect [ 24.598700 749.713013 209.501999 760.713013 ]
>>

% Dashed green line
22 0 obj
<<
    /Type Annot
    /Subtype Line
    /BS << /D [ 4 4 ] /S D /W 5 >>
    /C [ 0 1 0 ]
    /L [ 28.869200 717.310974 202.772995 717.310974 ]
    /Rect [ 21.369200 709.810974 210.272995 724.810974 ]
>>

% Blue line with an arrowhead at the end
24 0 obj
<<
    /Type Annot
    /Subtype Line
    /BS << /W 3 >>
    /C [ 0 0 1 ]
```

```
/L [ 30.098700 687.211975 200.658005 687.211975 ]
/LE [ None OpenArrow ]
/Rect [ 23.598700 680.711975 207.158005 693.711975 ]
    >>
```

Polygons and polylines

While a single line is useful, in most cases a series of lines that connect to each other creating an open (*polyline*) or closed (*polygon*) shape will address more cases for drawing and markup of the content on the page. As with line and square annotations, the LE, BS, BE, IC, and C keys serve to provide some styling attributes.

 For polyline annotations, the value of the IC key is used to fill only the line ending. However, for *Polygon* annotations, the value of the IC key is used to fill the entire shape, much as the F operator would fill a shape in a content stream.

The actual points along the shape are specified as an array value for the Vertices key, with alternating horizontal and vertical coordinates.

 As with QuadPoints, even though a Vertices array is more specific than the Rect, the Rect is always required to be present.

One other key that is specific to polyline and polygon annotations is the IT key, which provides the *intent* of the object. It takes a name value of PolygonCloud, PolyLineDimension, or PolygonDimension. Figure 6-5 provides a few exmaples of polygon and polyline annotations.

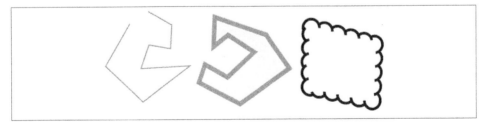

Figure 6-5. Examples of polygon and polyline annotations

```
% red polyline (as the shape is open)
105 0 obj
<<
    /Type Annot
```

```
    /Subtype PolyLine
    /C [ 1 0 0 ]
    /Rect [ 272.049011 536.856018 372.549011 640.978027 ]
    /Vertices [ 301.295013 626.216003 273.049011 578.414978
                316.505005 537.856018 371.549011 578.414978
                314.332001 575.518005 323.747009 602.315979
                349.096985 597.969971 350.545013 625.492004
                350.545013 624.768005 323.023010 639.978027 ]
>>

% polygon stroked in (RGB) green and filled in (CMYK) yellow
107 0 obj
<<
    /Type Annot
    /Subtype Polygon
    /BS << /W 5 >>
    /C [ 0 1 0 ]
    /IC [ 0 0 1 0 ]
    /Rect [ 376.688995 529.958984 491.707001 638.458984 ]
    /Vertices [ 399.071014 600.143005 415.729004 613.179993
                446.148010 593.624023 415.005005 565.377991
                388.931000 579.862976 381.688995 559.583984
                429.489990 534.958984 486.707001 574.794006
                459.908997 613.179993 400.519989 633.458984
                399.071014 600.143005 ]
>>

% polygon stroked in (grayscale) black
109 0 obj
<<
    /Type Annot
    /Subtype Polygon
    /BE << /I 2 /S C >>
    /BS << /W 3 >>                        ,
    /C [ 0 ]
    /IT PolygonCloud
    /Rect [ 497.958008 525.330994 598.528015 633.752014 ]
    /Vertices [ 512.057007 621.146973 585.932007 601.591003
                583.034973 537.856018 510.608002 553.789978
                510.608002 582.036011 512.057007 621.146973 ]
>>
```

Ink

As flexible as the polygon and polyline annotations are, sometimes a completely free-form drawing connecting a series of arbitrary points is needed. Additionally, polygon and polyline segments are connected via straight lines, but sometimes a curve is necessary. For that purpose, the *ink* annotation is provided in PDF.

As with the other annotation types we've seen, the LE, BS, and C keys serve to provide some styling attributes (see Example 6-1). The points themselves are stored in an array that is the value of the `InkList` key, and since it is usually a very long list, it's quite common (though not required) to have the list as a separate indirect object.

Example 6-1. Examples of ink annotations

```
% red ink
141 0 obj
<<
    /C [ 1 0 0 ]
    /InkList 126 0 R
    /Rect [ 40.283199 451.471008 158.264999 517.778992 ]
    /Subtype Ink
    /Type Annot
>>

% green ink
143 0 obj
<<
    /BS << /W 5 >>
    /C [ 0 1 0 ]
    /InkList 192 0 R
    /Rect [ 186.205994 427.546997 299.170013 516.556030 ]
    /Subtype Ink
    /Type Annot
>>

% magenta ink
145 0 obj
<<
    /BS << /W 3 >>
    /C [ 0 1 0 0]
    /InkList 209 0 R
    /Rect [ 323.010986 408.593994 479.394989 506.535004 ]
    /Subtype Ink
    /Type Annot
>>

126 0 obj
[
    41.2832 487.808 42.0075 488.532 42.731700000000004 489.256 44.1803 490.705
    45.6288 492.154 47.0773 493.602 49.9744 496.499 52.8715 498.672 55.7685
    57.9413 503.018 61.5627 506.639 65.184 508.812 68.0811 510.984 69.5296
    70.2539 513.882 72.4267 515.33 72.4267 516.054 73.8752 516.779 73.1509
    72.4267 513.882 70.2539 511.709 68.0811 507.363 64.4597 503.018 60.1141
    56.4928 493.602 55.0443 487.808 52.8715 483.462 52.1472 479.841 52.1472
```

```
    52.8715 476.22 54.32 475.495 55.7685 475.495 58.6656 476.22 62.2869 478.392
    66.6325 480.565 70.2539 482.738 73.8752 484.911 75.3237 487.808 76.7723
    77.4965 492.154 77.4965 493.602 77.4965 494.326 77.4965 493.602 76.7723
    % Lots more numbers would go here...
]

192 0 obj
[
    348.372 500.845 348.372 500.12 348.372 499.396 348.372 498.672 348.372
    348.372 497.223 347.648 496.499 346.924 495.775 346.199 495.775 345.475
    344.751 493.602 343.302 493.602 342.578 492.154 341.854 491.429 341.13
    340.405 489.981 339.681 489.981 338.957 489.981 338.233 489.981 336.784
    336.06 490.705 334.611 491.429 333.163 492.154 330.99 493.602 330.266
    328.817 494.326 328.093 495.051 327.369 495.051 326.644 495.775 326.644
    326.644 497.223 326.644 497.948 326.644 498.672 328.093 498.672 328.817
    330.266 500.12 332.438 500.845 333.887 500.845 336.784 501.569 339.681
    344.027 502.293 348.372 502.293 351.994 502.293 356.339 502.293 359.236
    362.133 502.293 364.306 502.293 366.479 502.293 368.652 501.569 369.376
    370.825 498.672 371.549 497.223 372.273 495.775 372.997 494.326 372.997
    % Lots more numbers would go here...
]

209 0 obj
[
    191.206 504.466 191.206 503.742 191.206 502.293 191.206 500.845 191.206
    191.931 496.499 191.931 492.878 192.655 487.808 193.379 484.911 193.379
    194.828 478.392 194.828 476.22 194.828 474.047 195.552 473.323 196.276
    197.001 470.426 197.001 471.15 197.725 471.874 197.725 474.047 197.725
    198.449 479.117 199.173 482.738 200.622 485.635 202.07 489.981 204.243
    205.692 498.672 207.14 503.018 209.313 506.639 210.762 508.812 210.762
    210.762 510.984 211.486 510.984 211.486 508.812 211.486 505.915 211.486
    211.486 497.223 211.486 492.878 211.486 487.808 211.486 482.738 211.486
    212.21 473.323 212.934 468.977 213.659 467.528 213.659 466.08 214.383
    % Lots more numbers would go here...
]
```

Stamps Markup

When the drawing annotation types are not rich enough to represent the graphics that
are to be drawn—for example, if you'd like to include a raster image (as discussed in
Chapter 3)—the *stamp* annotation is the choice. It is in some ways the simplest annotation to create, as the annotation dictionary only requires the Type and Subtype keys
from the standard dictionary. However, what makes it complex is that it also requires
an AP key and its associated appearance stream (see "Appearance Streams" on page 88).
Fortunately, an appearance stream is simply a form XObject (see "Vector Images" on
page 58). Figure 6-6 demonstrates a stamp annotation.

Figure 6-6. Sample stamp annotation

```
25 0 obj
<<
    /AP << /N 18 0 R >>
    /CA    0.5        % set the opacity to 50%
    /Rect [ 109.597 104.905 206.597 201.905 ]
    /Subtype Stamp
    /Type Annot
>>


18 0 obj
<<
    /Type /XObject
    /Subtype /Form
    /BBox    [ 0 0 147 147 ]
    /FormType 1
    /Length 74    % or whatever it really is
    /Matrix    [ 1 0 0 1 0 0 ]
    /Resources << /XObject << /FRM 20 0 R >> >>    % refers to subsequent XOb-
ject stream
q
0 0 147 147 re
W n
q
0 0 147 147 re
W n
1 0 0 1 73.5 73.5 cm
/FRM Do
Q
Q
endstream
endobj


20 0 obj
<<
    /Type /XObject
    /Subtype /Form
    /BBox    [ 249 421 396 568 ]
    /FormType 1
    /Length 348    % or whatever it really is
    /Matrix    [ 1 0 0 1 -322.5 -494.5 ]
```

```
stream
0 0 1 0 k
0 0 0 1 K
0 J 0 j 6 w 4 M []0 d
/GS2 gs
1 i
322.787 425.358 m
360.798 425.358 391.612 456.173 391.612 494.184 c
391.612 532.194 360.798 563.009 322.787 563.009 c
284.777 563.009 253.962 532.194 253.962 494.184 c
253.962 456.173 284.777 425.358 322.787 425.358 c
b
0 g
353.747 517.033 m
353.747 522.313 350.147 526.153 345.107 526.153 c
340.067 526.153 335.987 522.073 335.987 517.273 c
335.987 512.473 340.307 508.633 344.867 508.633 c
349.427 508.633 353.747 512.233 353.747 517.033 c
f
307.08 517.033 m
307.08 522.313 303.48 526.153 298.44 526.153 c
293.4 526.153 289.32 522.073 289.32 517.273 c
289.32 512.473 293.64 508.633 298.2 508.633 c
302.76 508.633 307.08 512.233 307.08 517.033 c
f
1 J
278.216 481.06 m
284 468.393 298.267 456.076 323 456.076 c
347.733 456.076 362 469.06 367.783 481.06 c
S
endstream
endobj
```

In the preceding example, a form XObject references another form
XObject. This is not a requirement for the stamp annotation, but it is
a common pattern.

In this example the annotation dictionary contains a CA key that specifies the amount
of opacity to apply to the entire appearance stream of the annotation when it is drawn
on the page.

The other interesting thing that this example demonstrates is that even the form XObject
used in an annotation's appearance stream can refer to additional resources, including
any number of subsequent and nested form XObjects.

Text Annotations and Pop-ups

A *text* annotation is used to represent a "sticky note" that is placed at a specific place on the PDF page. The text of the note is the string value for the Contents key in the annotation dictionary. Although a standard appearance stream should be used to provide the drawing instructions, it is also possible to just provide a Name key with a value that gives the PDF viewer a clue what icon to use. ISO 32000-1, Table 172 lists the possible names that a PDF viewer is required to provide for. Some common icons used for those names are the following:

Icon	Name
◯	Comment
⚷	Key
▤	Note
⑦	Help
△	NewParagraph
⑪	Paragraph
∧	Insert

The *pop-up* annotation is a special type of annotation that exists to allow the association of a string of text with markup annotations. It doesn't have an appearance of its own, but instead has a parent key in its annotation dictionary that points to another annotation, which is one of the markup annotations. This parent annotation provides the actual appearance stream for the annotation, if any. Additionally, the parent annotation's dictionary contains a Contents key whose value is a string that specifies the text to be displayed in the "note."

In addition to the Parent annotation, the pop-up annotation dictionary can also contain an Open key whose Boolean value determines if the viewer should show it open or closed by default (see Figure 6-7).

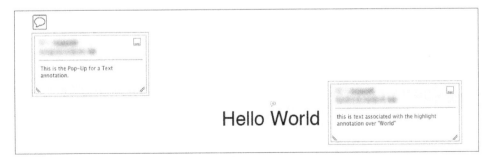

Figure 6-7. Text and pop-up examples

```
19 0 obj
<<
    /Popup 20 0 R
    /Name /Comment
    /Contents (This is the pop-up for a text annotation)
    /Type /Annot
    /Rect [261.52 558.755 279.52 576.755]
    /Subtype /Text
>>
endobj

20 0 obj
<<
    /Parent 19 0 R
    /Subtype /Popup
    /Type /Annot
    /Rect [287.427 457.785 467.428 578.222]
    /Open true
>>
endobj

21 0 obj
<<
    /Subtype /Highlight
    /C [1 1 0]
    /Popup 22 0 R
    /QuadPoints [321.343 622.344 384.006 622.344 321.343 594.6 384.006 594.6]
      /Contents (this is text associated with the highlight annotation over
"World")
    /Type /Annot
    /Rect [313.937 593.733 391.412 623.211]
>>
endobj

22 0 obj
<<
    /Parent 21 0 R
    /Subtype /Popup
    /Type /Annot
    /Rect [395.62 592.048 575.62 712.485]
    /Open true
>>
endobj
```

Non-Markup Annotations

Table 6-3. Non-markup annotations

Annotation type	Description
3D	3D annotation
FileAttachment	File attachment

Annotation type	Description
Link	Link annotation
Movie	Movie annotation
Popup	Pop-up annotation
PrinterMark	Printer's mark annotation
Screen	Screen annotation
Sound	Sound
TrapNet	Trap network annotation
Watermark	Watermark annotation
Widget	Widget annotation

Non-markup annotations can themselves be divided into a number of subcategories:

Interactive elements

> We've already seen link annotations in our discusion about GoTo actions in Example 5-3, and widget annotations have an entire chapter (Chapter 7) dedicated to them.

Multimedia content

> These annotation types enable media (including videos, sound, and 3D) to be displayed and interacted with inside of a PDF. They are all discussed in Chapter 9.

Print production

> PDF supports two annotations types for the print industry, *PrinterMark* and *TrapNet*. As no one uses these, this will be all we'll say about them.

Other

> There are two other types of annotations that don't fall into any of these categories: *FileAttachment* and *Watermark*.
>
> File attachment annotations are one way to embed/attach files to a PDF, much like you would with an email message. These are covered in Chapter 8.
>
> The watermark annotation was introduced into PDF for use by engineers as a way to designate a special graphic that does not scale when printed. They aren't used very much and so won't get any coverage here either.

What's Next

In this chapter, we learned about annotation. Next you will look at a specific type of annotation, the widget type, which serves as the basis for PDF forms.

CHAPTER 7

AcroForms

This chapter will go into detail on a special type of annotation: the *widget* annotation that is the building block for PDF forms.

PDF 1.2 introduced the concept of an *interactive form* (a collection of fields that can be used to gather information interactively from a user) to the PDF format. There will be at most one single, global form in the PDF; it can contain any number of fields, which can appear on any combination of pages.

> Interactive forms should not be confused with form XObjects (discussed in "Vector Images" on page 58). Despite the similarity of their names, the two are different, unrelated types of objects.

The Interactive Form Dictionary

The document's interactive form is described using an *interactive form dictionary*, which is the value of the AcroForm key found in the document catalog dictionary.

> Because that is the name of the key, the interactive form dictionary is frequently referred to as the *AcroForm dictionary* and the type of form as an *AcroForm*.

This dictionary has only one required key, Fields, which specifies an array of field dictionaries that represent the fields in the form. However, there are a few common optional fields that you may need to specify for some of your forms:

DR

When creating the appearance streams for your fields, you may wish to refer to some resources shared by one or more fields. The resource dictionary specified by this key serves to provide that information, much as the page resource dictionary does for page content. If the DR key is present, its value (of type dictionary) needs to include a Font key. The value of Font is the resource name and font to be used as a default font for displaying text in fields.

NeedAppearances

This field should only be present and set to true when one or more fields in the form do not have an appearance stream. It is intended as a clue for a viewer to forceably rebuild such streams; however, many viewers do not respect this. It is therefore recommended to always provide the appearance streams for each field.

XFA

PDF 1.5 introduced a special type of form called XFA (eXtensible Form Architecture) that uses an XML grammar to describe the form rather than native PDF syntax. The value of this key, if present, is an array of XML fragments based on the XFA grammar (*http://www.adobe.com/go/xfa_specifications*).

The Field Dictionary

The field dictionary specifies the details of each field in a document's interactive form. Fields can be organized hierarchically and can inherit attributes from their ancestors in the hierarchy. A field that has children that are fields is called a *nonterminal field*. A field that does not have children, such as a simple button or text field, is called a *terminal field*. Child fields are specified in an array of field dictionaries that is the value of a Kids key, while a child's parent is specified via the Parent key.

Every field has to have a class associated with it via an FT key in the field dictionary (or inherited from a parent field). There are four possible values for the class of a field:

Btn

Button fields, which include push buttons, checkboxes, and radio buttons.

Tx

Text fields into which a user can enter text.

Ch

Choice fields such as scrollable lists, combo boxes, or pop-up menus.

Sig

Signature fields to enable digital signatures for PDF.

Since the purpose of a field is to gather information from a user, it needs a way to store that value. That storage location is the value of the V key in the field dictionary. The type of value and how it relates to the field differs based on the type of field.

Field Names

While not required, most fields have names associated with them. In fact, a field can have up to three different names, each used in a different context.

The T key in the field dictionary consists of a text string value that defines the field's partial field name. A field's fully qualified name is never explicitly defined in the PDF but instead is dynamically constructed from the partial field names of the field and all of its ancestors. For a field with no parent, the partial and fully qualified names are the same. For a field that is the child of another field, the fully qualified name is constructed by appending the child field's partial name to the parent's fully qualified name, separated by a period (2Eh). Because the period is used as a separator for fully qualified names, a partial name cannot contain a period character.

 For example, if a field with the partial field name UserInfo has a child whose partial name is Address, which in turn has a child with the partial name ZipCode, the fully qualified name of this last field is *User-Info.Address.ZipCode*.

When preparing a PDF that may be processed by a screen reader or other assistive technology, it is important to provide a TU key for each field. The value of this key is a text string that is used instead of the field's partial or fully qualified name to identify it to the user.

The third name that a field might have is its *export name*—a name used when exporting the data to a file. The TM key's string value will be exported as the name that is associated with the field's value when it is exported to various formats. If not present, then the field's partial name will be used.

Field Flags

A field dictionary may contain (or may inherit) an Ff key whose value is an unsigned 32-bit integer composed of a series of "bit flags" or "bit positions" that specify various characteristics of the field. These bit positions within the flag word are numbered from 1 (low-order) to 32 (high-order). There are three flags (listed in Table 7-1) that are common to all classes of fields, but there are also many flags that apply only to specific field classes. All undefined flag bits are considered reserved and are set to 0 by a PDF writer.

Table 7-1. Standard field flags

Bit position	Name	Meaning
1	ReadOnly	If set, the user may not change the value of the field. This flag is useful for fields whose values are computed or imported from a database.
2	Required	If set, the field must have a value at the time it is exported by a SubmitForm action.
3	NoExport	If set, the field may not be exported by a SubmitForm action.

Fields and Annotations

One thing that hasn't been mentioned yet is how to define which page the field belongs on and where to draw it on the page. The field dictionary does not provide for any keys that would define these things, whereas the annotation dictionary that we learned about in "Annotation Dictionaries" on page 87 does. As such, we are going to combine these two things to solve our problem.

A widget annotation is created for each field that is to be drawn, and then associated (as with any other annotation) to the page on which it will appear. This means that a single dictionary will contain keys from both a field dictionary and an annotation dictionary. If the field is the parent of a group (such as a radio button group), and the grouping itself has no visual representation and is therefore not drawn on a page, then it will be a standard field dictionary without any annotation extras.

This merged dictionary is only necessary/required for any form field that will be displayed on a page.

Example 7-1 shows a widget annotation that includes both annotation information (e.g., Rect, AP) and field information (e.g., FT, Ff).

Example 7-1. Example field and widget annotation

```
16 0 obj
<<
    /F 4
    /Type /Annot
    /Rect [27.014 749.644 99.014 769.644]
    /FT /Btn
    /Ff 65536
    /Subtype /Widget
    /T (PushButton)
    /AP << /N 42 0 R >>
>>
endobj
```

Field Classes

As mentioned earlier, every field must have a class associated with it. The field types include button, text, choice, and signature fields.

Button Fields

A button field represents an interactive control or element on the page that the user can "press" with a mouse or other pointing device. There are three types of button fields (see Figure 7-1):

Pushbutton
> A field with the Pushbutton bit set to 1 that does not have any value (and thus no V key in its dictionary)

Checkbox
> A field that toggles between two states, on and off, and has both the Pushbutton and RadioButton flags clear. The states refer to the names of the appearance streams associated with the field and are also the name value(s) for the V key.

Radio button
> One of a set of related buttons, of which only one can be on at a time. As with checkboxes, each button can have two states (on and off), and they are used in the same way. These fields will have the Pushbutton flag clear but the RadioButton flag set.

For button fields, bits 15, 16, 17, and 26 of the field flags indicate the intended behavior, as described in Table 7-2.

Table 7-2. Button field flags

Bit position	Name	Meaning
15	NoToggleToOff (radio buttons only)	If set, exactly one radio button shall be selected at all times; selecting the currently selected button has no effect. If clear, clicking the selected button deselects it, leaving no button selected.
16	Radio	If set, the field is a set of radio buttons; if clear, the field is a checkbox. This flag may be set only if the Pushbutton flag is clear.
17	Pushbutton	If set, the field is a pushbutton that does not retain a permanent value.
26	RadiosInUnison	If set, a group of radio buttons within a radio button field that use the same value for the on state will turn on and off in unison; that is, if one is checked, they are all checked. If clear, the buttons are mutually exclusive (the same behavior as HTML radio buttons).

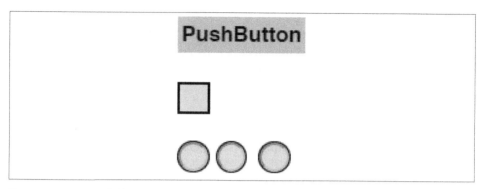

Figure 7-1. Example buttons

```
% Document catalog
12 0 obj
<<
    /Metadata 2 0 R
    /Type /Catalog
    /Pages 9 0 R
    /AcroForm 22 0 R
    /Outlines 6 0 R
>>
endobj

% AcroForm dictionary
22 0 obj
<<
    /Fields [16 0 R 17 0 R 24 0 R]
>>
endobj

% Pushbutton field
16 0 obj
<<
    /F 4
    /Type /Annot
    /Rect [27.014 749.644 99.014 769.644]
    /FT /Btn
    /Ff 65536
    /Subtype /Widget
    /T (PushButton)
    /AP << /N 42 0 R >>
>>
endobj

% Checkbox field
17 0 obj
<<
    /Type /Annot
    /Rect [27.014 715.314 45.014 733.314]
```

```
    /FT /Btn
    /AS /Off          % default state is Off (unchecked)
    /Subtype /Widget
    /F 4
    /T (CheckBox)
    /AP <<
        /N << /Yes 38 0 R /Off 37 0 R >>
        /D << /Yes 41 0 R /Off 40 0 R >>
    >>
>>
endobj

% Radio button #3
18 0 obj
<<
    /F 4
    /Rect [27.014 682.711 45.014 700.711]
    /Parent 24 0 R     % this is the radio button group...
    /AS /Off           % default state is Off (unchecked)
    /Subtype /Widget
    /Type /Annot
    /AP <<
        /N << /2 33 0 R /Off 34 0 R >>
        /D << /2 35 0 R /Off 36 0 R >>
    >>
>>
endobj

% Radio button #2
20 0 obj
<<
    /F 4
    /Rect [48.7541 682.711 66.7541 700.711]
    /Parent 24 0 R     % this is the radio button group...
    /AS /Off           % default state is Off (unchecked)
    /Subtype /Widget
    /Type /Annot
    /AP <<
        /N << /1 29 0 R /Off 30 0 R >>
        /D << /1 31 0 R /Off 32 0 R >>
    >>
>>
endobj

% Radio button #1
21 0 obj
<<
    /F 4
    /Type /Annot
    /Rect [73.1377 682.711 91.1377 700.711]
    /Parent 24 0 R       % this is the radio button group...
    /AS /0               % default state is 0, which is On
```

```
    /Subtype /Widget
    /AP <<
        /N << /0 25 0 R /Off 26 0 R >>
        /D << /0 27 0 R /Off 28 0 R >>
    >>
>>
endobj

% this is the radio button grouping field
24 0 obj
<<
    /Kids [21 0 R 20 0 R 18 0 R]
    /FT /Btn
    /Opt [(RadioButton1) (RadioButton1) (RadioButton1)]
    /Ff 49152
    /T (RadioButton)
>>
endobj
```

Text Fields

Text fields are areas on the page where arbitrary text/strings can be entered either by a user or programmatically by software. The text is normally only drawn in a single font, size, and color along a single line; however, various flags and additional keys can be supplied in the field dictionary to enable the text to span multiple lines (wrapping accordingly), or use rich text formatting, or both. Figure 7-2 shows a few examples.

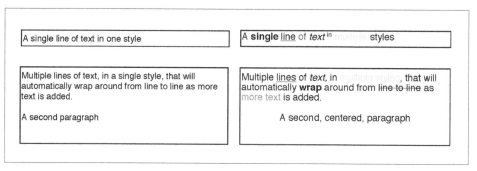

Figure 7-2. Text fields

Plain text

The text string (or stream) that represents the value of the field is stored as the value of the V key in the field dictionary. When creating the appearance for the field, the text is normally drawn in a single style (font, size, color, and so forth), which is defined by the value of the DA key. Example 7-2 shows a few examples of text fields.

Example 7-2. Simple text fields

```
16 0 obj
<<
    /DA (/Helv 12 Tf 0 g)
    /F 4
    /FT Tx
    /Rect [ 9.526760 680.078003 297.527008 702.078003 ]
    /Subtype /Widget
    /Type /Annot
    /T (SimpleText)
    /V (A single line of text in one style)
>>
endobj

17 0 obj
<<
    /DA /Helv 12 Tf 0 g
    /F 4
    /FT Tx
    /Ff 4096
    /Rect [ 8.184650 550.416992 296.184998 653.090027 ]
    /Subtype /Widget
    /Type /Annot
    /T (MultilineText)
    /V (Multiple lines of text in a single style will automatically wrap
        around from line to line as more text is added to a second paragraph)
>>
endobj
```

Rich text

If the text value of the field should be displayed in multiple styles, then a rich text string is provided as the value of the RV key in the field dictionary and bit 26 of the text field flags should be set. A rich text string is a fully formed XML document that conforms to the grammar defined for rich text in the XFA specification (*http://www.adobe.com/go/ xfa_specifications*), which is based on specific subsets of the XHTML 1.0 (*http:// www.w3.org/TR/xhtml1/*) and CSS2 (*http://bit.ly/GzHCYJ*) standards.

The <body> element is the root of the document, which is then divided up into paragraphs (<p>) and spans (<span>) that are styled using standard CSS attributes such as font-family and color. Example 7-3 shows an example of a rich text field.

Example 7-3. A rich text field

```
20 0 obj
<<
    /F 4
    /FT Tx
    /Ff 33554432
    /Rect [ 312.427002 680.749023 600.427002 702.749023 ]
    /Subtype /Widget
```

```
    /Type /Annot
    /T (RichText)
    /V (A single line of text in multiple styles)
    /RV (<?xml version="1.0"?> \
        <body xfa:APIVersion="Acroform:2.7.0.0" xfa:spec="2.1" \
        xmlns="http://www.w3.org/1999/xhtml" \
        xmlns:xfa="http://www.xfa.org/schema/xfa-data/1.0/"><p \
        style="margin-top:0pt;margin-bottom:0pt;text-valign:top;font- \
        family:Helvetica;font-size:13pt"><span>A </span><span \
        style="font-weight:bold">single</span><span \
        style="font-weight:normal"> </span><span \
        style="font-weight:normal;text-decoration:underline">line</span>< \
        span style="font-weight:normal;text-decoration:none"> </span>< \
        </span><span \
        style="color:#0000ff;font-weight:normal;text-decoration:none">of< \
        /span><span \
        style="color:#000000;font-weight:normal;text-decoration:none"> \
        </span><span \
        style="color:#000000;font-weight:normal;font-style:italic;text- \
        decoration:none">text</span><span \
        style="color:#000000;font-weight:normal;font-style:normal;text- \
        decoration:none"> </span><span \
        style="vertical-align:4.03pt;font-size:8.58pt;color:#000000;font- \
        weight:normal;font-style:normal;text-decoration:none">in</span>< \
        span \
        style="vertical-align:baseline;color:#000000;font-weight:normal; \
        font-style:normal;text-decoration:none"> </span><span \
        style="vertical-align:baseline;color:#00ff00;font-weight:normal; \
        font-style:normal;text-decoration:none">multiple</span><span \
        style="vertical-align:baseline;color:#000000;font-weight:normal; \
        font-style:normal;text-decoration:none"> styles</span></p></body>)
>>
endobj


21 0 obj<<
    /F 4
    /FT Tx
    /Ff 33558528
    /Rect [ 311.756012 550.416992 599.755981 653.090027 ]
    /Subtype /Widget
    /Type /Annot
    /T (MultilineRichText)
    /V (Multiple lines of text, in multiple styles,\
        automatically wrap around from line to line as more text is added. \
        A second, centered, paragraph)
    /RV (<?xml version="1.0"?>
    <body xfa:APIVersion="Acroform:2.7.0.0" xfa:spec="2.1" \
    xmlns="http://www.w3.org/1999/xhtml" \
    xmlns:xfa="http://www.xfa.org/schema/xfa-data/1.0/"><p \
    style="margin-top:0pt;margin-bottom:0pt;font-family:Helvetica;font- \
    size:13pt"><span>Multiple </span><span \
```

```
style="text-decoration:underline">lines</span><span \
style="text-decoration:none"> of </span><span \
style="font-style:italic;text-decoration:none">text,</span><span \
style="font-style:normal;text-decoration:none"> in </span><span \
style="color:#00ff00;font-style:normal;text-decoration:none">multiple \
styles</span><span \
style="color:#000000;font-style:normal;text-decoration:none">, that \
will automatically </span><span \
style="color:#000000;font-weight:bold;font-style:normal;text- \
decoration:none">wrap</span><span \
style="color:#000000;font-weight:normal;font-style:normal;text- \
decoration:none"> around from </span><span \
style="color:#000000;font-weight:normal;font-style:normal;text- \
decoration:line-through">line to line</span><span \
style="color:#000000;font-weight:normal;font-style:normal;text- \
decoration:none"> as </span><span \
style="color:#ff0000;font-weight:normal;font-style:normal;text- \
decoration:none">more text</span><span \
style="color:#000000;font-weight:normal;font-style:normal;text- \
decoration:none"> is added.</span></p><p \
style="margin-top:0pt;margin-bottom:0pt;font-family:Helvetica;font- \
size:13pt"> </p><p \
style="margin-top:0pt;margin-bottom:0pt;text-align:center;font-family \
:Helvetica;font-size:13pt"><span>A second, centered, \
paragraph</span></p></body>)
>>
endobj
```

Text field flags

ISO 32000-1, Table 228 lists all of the field flags that can be specified on a text field, but the most commonly used are the following:

Bit 13

> The multiline flag is set when the text value of the field should be wrapped to the rect of the annotation.

Bit 14

> The password flag specifies that the value of this field is never to be drawn nor stored in the PDF, but only maintained locally for the purposes of data submission.

Bit 26

> The rich text flag specifies that the value of this field is not just a simple string, but is actually richly styled text.

Choice Fields

A choice field is used to present a user with a choice of multiple options from which she can select one or more to become the value of the field.

MultiSelect flag

Normally a choice field only allows a single item in the list of options/choices to be chosen by the user. However, there are times when the selection of multiple items can be useful. To enable this, the multiselect flag (bit 22) of the field flags is set.

Options

The list of text strings that will be displayed in the field as the choices from which the user can select are stored in an array as the value of the Opt key in the field dictionary. In most cases, the array is a simple array of just text strings; however, if the export name of a given text string needs to be different, then that element of the array will itself be an array of two elements—the text string to be displayed followed by the export name. Example 7-4 illustrates both approaches.

Example 7-4. Examples of options

```
% Simple options
/Opt [ (France) (Belgium) (Germany) (United Kingdom) (Spain) ]

% Options with alternate export names
/Opt [ (France) (Belgium) [(Germany) (DE)] [(United Kingdom) (UK)] (Spain) ]
```

Values

The value, as with other field types, is stored as the value of the V key in the field dictionary. However, when the multiselect flag is set, the value is of type array instead of a text string.

 The value of V may also be of type null, which is the default, to indicate that nothing has been chosen from the options.

The list of selected items will be stored as the value of the I key in the field dictionary. The value will consist of a list of integers representing the (zero-based) indices of the items that are selected. Normally this is used only for fields with the multiselect flag set, but it can be used for single-selection fields as well.

 If the items listed in the value of I differ from those in value of V in the field dictionary, the V entry will take precedence.

Scrolling lists

The default type of choice field is the scrolling list (Example 7-5), which displays the list of items in a scrollable (if there are too many to show all at once) list. A user can either have nothing selected or at least one item selected.

Example 7-5. Scrolling list

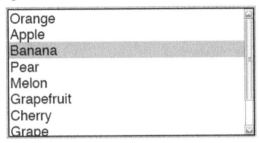

```
16 0 obj
<<
    /DV (Prune)          % the default value if another is not specified
    /F 4
    /FT Ch
    /I [ 2 ]
        /Opt [ (Orange) (Apple) (Banana) (Pear) (Melon) (Grapefruit) (Cherry)
               (Grape) (Prune) ]
    /Rect [ 59.053501 606.116028 275.135986 716.169983 ]
    /Subtype /Widget
    /T (ListBox)
    /Type /Annot
    /V (Banana)
>>
endobj
```

Combo boxes

Rather than taking up a lot of the page with the full list of items, they can instead be presented in a smaller combo box from which the users can select the items they wish (Example 7-6). If bit 18 of the field flags is set, the choice field will be presented as a combo box.

Example 7-6. Combo box

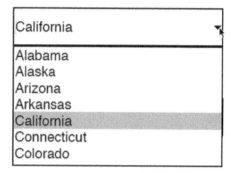

```
17 0 obj
<<
    /DV (California)
    /F 4
    /FT Ch
    /Ff 131072
    /I [ 4 ]
    /Opt [ (Alabama) (Alaska) (Arizona) (Arkansas) (California) (Connecticut)
           (Colorado) ]
    /Rect [ 341.571014 682.617004 526.112976 715.499023 ]
    /Subtype /Widget
    /T (Dropdown)
    /Type /Annot
    /V (California)
>>
endobj
```

Editable combo boxes

Sometimes it is not possible to include all the possible choices in a list, and it will be necessary for the users to enter their own values (Example 7-7). Setting bit 19 of the field flags makes the value of the combo box editable.

Example 7-7. Editable combo box

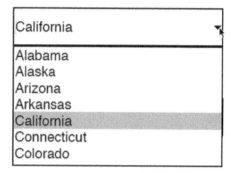

```
<<
    /DV (Germany)
    /F 4
```

```
/FT Ch
/Ff 393216
/Opt [ (France) (Belgium) (Germany) (United Kingdom) (Spain) ]
/Rect [ 342.242004 606.116028 526.783997 638.997986 ]
/Subtype /Widget
/T (DropdownE)
/Type /Annot
/V (Slovakia)
>>
```

Signature Fields

A signature field provides a way to identify that a user should apply a digital or electronic signature to the PDF (see Figure 7-3). As such, the field can be thought of as being either signed or not signed. A signed signature field will have a V key in its field dictionary.

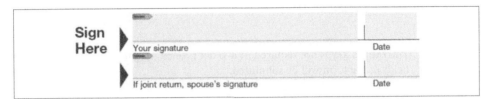

Figure 7-3. Two signature fields

Prior to the user actually signing the field, it serves as a placeholder on the page for where the graphical representation of the signature (if present) will be drawn, along with any information about the type of signature technologies that should be used at the time of signing.

 Signature fields that are not intended to be visible will have an annotation rectangle that has zero height and width or have either the Hidden bit or the NoView bit of the F key in their annotation dictionaries set.

The actual process of digitally signing or verifying a PDF is very complex and beyond the scope of this book. If you wish to read more about it, I highly recommend Bruno Lowagie's "Digital Signatures for PDF Documents" (*http://bit.ly/16D8mV5*).

Form Actions

In addition to the navigational actions, there are three types of actions that are specific to form fields: SubmitForm, ResetForm, and ImportData. Just as the navigational actions can be associated with bookmarks or links, these form-related actions can be as well. However, it is more common to associate them with a button field on the form.

SubmitForm

The SubmitForm action informs the PDF viewer to transmit the names and values of the specified fields to the specified URL in the specified format. This information is provided in the action dictionary, whose S key will have a value of SubmitForm.

The URL where the form data will be submitted is specified as a URL file specification, which is the value of the F key in the action dictionary.

The fields that are to be included in the submitted data are specified in the array value of the Fields key. Each element of the array can be either an indirect reference to a field dictionary or a text string representing the fully qualified name of a field. Elements of both kinds may be mixed in the same array.

 The Fields key is not required. If it is not present, that means that all fields of the form will be submitted.

Submission formats

PDF provides the specification of four different formats in which the form data can be submitted to the specified URL. The choice of format is determined by a series of flags that are specified as the value of the Flags key of the action dictionary:

FDF
> The Forms Data Format (FDF) is a subset of the PDF syntax that can be used to represent form data. It is described in ISO 32000-1, 12.7.7 and is the default format for data submission. To use this format, be sure that bits 3 (ExportFormat), 6 (XFDF), and 9 (SubmitPDF) are clear.

HTML
> This is the same format that HTML 4.01 (*http://www.w3.org/TR/REC-html40/*) uses to submit form data. To use this format, set bit 3 (ExportFormat) and be sure to keep bits 6 (XFDF) and 9 (SubmitPDF) clear.

XFDF
> The XML Forms Data Format (XFDF) is a version of FDF based on XML. XFDF is described in an Adobe technical note (*http://adobe.ly/14XTxsN*). To use this format, set bit 6 (XFDF) and be sure to keep bits 3 (ExportFormat) and 9 (SubmitPDF) clear.

PDF

With this format, the entire document is submitted rather than individual fields and values. To use this format, set bit 9 (`SubmitPDF`) and be sure to keep bits 3 (`ExportFormat`) and 6 (`XFDF`) clear.

Example 7-8 shows an example `SubmitForm` action.

Example 7-8. SubmitForm action

```
<<
    /F 4
    /FT Btn
    /Ff 65536
    /Rect [ 358.347992 725.026001 430.347992 745.026001 ]
    /Subtype /Widget
    /T (Submit)
    /Type /Annot
    /A <<
        /S SubmitForm
        /Fields [ (Address) (By) (Date) (Email) (Name) (TelNum) (Title) ]
        % since there is no *Flags* key that means use the default, FDF
    >>
>>
```

ResetForm

The `ResetForm` action is quite similar to the `SubmitForm` action in that it operates on a list of fields provided in the `Fields` key of the action dictionary. However, instead of the PDF viewer submitting the data of the specified fields to a specified URL, the value (V) of each field is reset to the value of its DV (Default Value) key. The S key in the action dictionary will have a value of `ResetForm`.

If present, the value of the `Flags` key can be only 0 or 1. A value of 0 (or the key not being present) means that the list of fields in `Fields` are the fields that should be reset. A value of 1 means that these are the fields that should not be reset (and to reset all others). Example 7-9 illustrates the latter approach.

Example 7-9. ResetForm action

```
<<
    /A <<
        /Fields [ (By_2) (Date_2) (Email_2) (Name_2) (TelNum_2) (Title_2) ]
        /Flags 1    % reset all BUT these...
        /S ResetForm
    >>
    /F 4
    /FT Btn
    /Ff 65536
    /Rect [ 447.501007 725.026001 519.500977 745.026001 ]
    /Subtype /Widget
```

```
    /T (Reset)
    /Type /Annot
>>
```

ImportData

The ImportData action enables the importing of the data from a specified FDF file into the fields of the PDF. The action dictionary has two required keys: the S key (with the value of ImportData) and the F key, whose value is a file specification dictionary indicating where the FDF data resides. It can be any type of file specification, including a URL file specification (see "URL File Specifications" on page 125).

What's Next

In this chapter, you learned about a special type of annotation, the widget annotation, which is the building block for PDF forms. Next you will learn about how to embed files in a PDF.

CHAPTER 8

Embedded Files

This chapter explains how a PDF can be used as a container for other files, much as a ZIP file can, while still providing rich page content to accompany them.

In most cases, file formats (such as *.docx* or *.xslx*) will be converted into PDF for distribution. However, sometimes it can be useful to have the original file as well. Unfortunately, there is a good chance that the two files will become disconnected, so having a way to embed or attach the original inside of the PDF is a useful capability. Additionally, you might choose to embed other files related to the PDF that aren't the actual content, such as XML data.

For these reasons and more, PDF supports the ability to embed other files inside of itself and then have them presented in the UI of the PDF viewer.

File Specifications

At the heart of embedding files is the *file specification dictionary*. This dictionary actually supports both embedded and referenced files, but we will focus strictly on the embedded form (see Figure 8-1). In order to ensure that the dictionary can be identified, it must contain a `Type` key whose value is `Filespec`. Additionally, there must be three other keys present in the dictionary: `F`, `UF`, and `EF` (see Example 8-1 for a sample).

The `F` key contains the name of the file in a special encoding specific to file specification strings (ISO 32000-1:2008, 7.11.2), which is the "standard encoding for the platform on which the document is being viewed." For most modern operating systems, that's UTF-8, but it isn't required to be so. However, the `UF` key contains the name encoded as standard 16-bit Unicode. The `EF` key refers to the embedded file dictionary, which is a simple dictionary with a single key, `F`, whose value is an embedded file stream where the actual data for the embedded file lives, along with some additional metadata about the file.

An optional Desc key can be provided whose value is a human-readable description of the file.

Name	Description	Modified	Size	Compressed size
Untitled.docx	Something I found on my disk	1/13/13 9:07:18 AM	11 KB	10 KB
mp3.סם בונ 04	Favorite Israeli music	8/9/10 7:02:01 AM	3,838 KB	3,839 KB

Figure 8-1. Two embedded files

Example 8-1. Sample file specification dictionaries

```
% file specification for a file with a simple ASCII name
20 0 obj
<<
    /F (Untitled.docx)
    /UF (Untitled.docx)
    /EF << /F 22 0 R >>
    /Type /Filespec
    /Desc (Something I found on my disk)
>>
endobj


% file specification for a file with a name requiring Unicode
31 0 obj
<<
    /F (04 ... ...mp3)
    /Type /Filespec
    /Desc (Favorite Israeli music)
    /EF << /F 32 0 R >>
    /UF (þÿ.0.4. .Ñ.Õ.Ý. .ä.Ý...m.p.3)     % 04 םפ בום.mp3
>>
endobj
```

Embedded File Streams

An embedded file stream is simply a stream object that contains the data for an embedded file. As such, it can be stored and compressed using filters (see "Stream Objects" on page 7) such as Flate—the same technology used in a ZIP file. A variety of additional information can be present in the embedded file stream's dictionary, such as the file's Internet media type (aka MIME type), as the value of the Subtype key. Other information, such as the date and time at which the file was created or last modified, can be included in the embedded file parameter dictionary (which is the value of the Params key). Example 8-2 shows an example of an embedded file stream.

Example 8-2. Example embedded file stream

```
32 0 obj
<<
    /Subtype /audio/mpeg
    /Filter /FlateDecode      % compressed using Flate/ZIP technology
    /Length 1000830           % encoded length
    /Params <<
        /ModDate (D:20100809110201)
        /CheckSum <1E2AFAC553A11A00E20A02774BA42EBF>
        /CreationDate (D:20130113152115-05'00')
        /Size 3930112      % decoded length
    >>
>>
stream
    % Flate-compressed stream data goes here....
endstream
endobj
```

> The value of the CheckSum key in the embedded file parameter dictionary is a 16-byte string that is the checksum of the bytes of the uncompressed embedded file, as calculated by applying the standard MD5 message-digest algorithm (*http://www.ietf.org/rfc/rfc1321.txt*) to the bytes of the embedded file stream.

A file specification and its associated embedded file stream are only one piece of the puzzle; it still needs to be connected to something in the PDF structure so that it can be found by the PDF viewer. If the file is associated with some specific content on a specific page, a *FileAttachment* annotation would be appropriate (see "FileAttachment Annotations" on page 126). However, if the file is more global to the document, the Embedded Files name tree would be the place (see "The EmbeddedFiles Name Tree" on page 127).

URL File Specifications

Although not used for embedded files, there is a special type of file specification called a URL that is used in other parts of PDF as the standard way to specify that the data stream of the file should be retrieved from a given uniform resource locator (URL).

To declare a file specification as a URL file specification, the FS key will have the value (of type Name) URL (see Example 8-3). In addition, the value of the F key will not be a file specification string, but instead will be a URL of the form defined in RFC 1738, "Uniform Resource Locators" (*http://www.ietf.org/rfc/rfc1738.txt*).

As the character-encoding requirements specified in RFC 1738 restrict the URL to 7-bit US ASCII, which is a strict subset of PDFDocEncoding, the value can also be considered to be in that encoding.

Example 8-3. Example URL file specification

```
<<
    /FS /URL
    /F (http://www.adobe.com/devnet/acrobat/pdfs/PDF32000_2008.pdf)
>>
```

Ways to Embed Files

Files can be connected to a PDF in two ways, depending on whether they are to be associated with specific content in a particular location or globally with the PDF as a whole. In the former case, we'll use file attachment annotations. In the latter case, the approach will be to add an EmbeddedFiles key to the document's name dictionary.

FileAttachment Annotations

The file attachment annotation is a simple type of annotation; it's similar to the text annotation, except that rather than having a Contents key with the text to be displayed, the Contents are some descriptive text about the file, such as the filename. It also contains an FS key that points to the file specification dictionary of the attached file (see "File Specifications" on page 123 for more), and its Subtype key has a value of FileAttachment.

Example 8-4 shows the result of placing a file attachment annotation that specifies the paperclip icon next to the text in *Hello World.pdf*.

Example 8-4. Example FileAttachment annotation

```
% the annotation object/dictionary
41 0 obj
<<
    /C [0.25 0.333328 1]
    /Type /Annot
    /Contents (world.jpg)
    /Name /Paperclip
    /Subtype /FileAttachment
    /FS 42 0 R
    /Rect [390.162 599.772 397.162 616.772]
>>
endobj

% the file specification dictionary
42 0 obj
```

```
<<
    /F (world.jpg)
    /Type /Filespec
    /UF (world.jpg)
    /EF << /F 43 0 R >>
>>
endobj

% and the embedded file stream
43 0 obj
<<
    /Subtype /image/jpeg
    /Length 25531
    /DL 20172
    /Params <<
        /ModDate (D:20121020024106-04'00')
        /CheckSum <19D579AB5B7C8F46B63C37F385707872>
        /CreationDate (D:20121020024106-04'00')
        /Size 20172
    >>
>>
stream
% Stream data goes here...
endstream
endobj
```

Hello World 📎

The EmbeddedFiles Name Tree

Embedded file streams are associated with the document as a whole by adding to the document's name dictionary an EmbeddedFiles key, whose value is a name tree. That name tree maps name strings to file specifications that refer to embedded file streams ("Embedded File Streams" on page 124) through their EF entries (see Example 8-5).

Example 8-5. Sample EmbeddedFile name tree

```
8 0 obj
<<
    /Type /Catalog
    /Names 16 0 R
    /PageMode /UseAttachments
    /Metadata 1 0 R          % not included in the sample
    /Pages 5 0 R             % not included in the sample
>>
endobj

16 0 obj
<<
    /EmbeddedFiles 17 0 R
```

```
>>
endobj

17 0 obj
<<
    /Names [
        (Some Embedded File) 21 0 R
        (Untitled.docx) 20 0 R
    ]
>>
endobj

20 0 obj
<<
    /F (Untitled.docx)
    /UF (Untitled.docx)
    /EF << /F 22 0 R >>
    /Type /Filespec
    /Desc (Something I found on my disk)
>>
endobj

21 0 obj
<<
    /F (Some Embedded File)
    /Type /Filespec
    /Desc (Something else on my disk)
    /EF << /F 32 0 R >>
    /UF (Some Embedded File)
>>
endobj
```

Collections

A PDF with embedded files is useful where the page content is the primary focus for the person who will read the document. However, sometimes you have a collection of documents that need to be grouped together, but none of them have any higher priority than another. Thus, the embedded files themselves are the focus. For example, it might be all the materials for a legal case or for bidding on an engineering job. In those cases, you want the PDF viewer to present the list of files and any associated metadata about them, rather than the normal view of a primary document's page content. It is for this purpose that the portable collections (or just "collections") feature of PDF is used. Figure 8-2 shows an example.

From	Subject	Date	Attachments	Size
	[PDFA-CC-Intern] PDF Association: Stay tuned in 2013!	Jan 9, 13 10:21:23 AM	1	32.81 KB
	Re: [PDFA-CC-tech] DigestMethod,DigestLocation and Dig	Jan 11, 13 4:42:26 PM	2	82.06 KB
	[PDFA-CC-tech] DigestMethod, DigestLocation and Dig	Jan 11, 13 1:46:28 PM	2	57.75 KB
	Re: [PDFA-CC-tech] DigestMethod,DigestLocation and Dig	Jan 11, 13 5:08:43 AM		32.23 KB
	[PDFA-CC-tech] DigestMethod, DigestLocation and Dig	Jan 10, 13 3:09:33 PM		28.25 KB
	Re: [PDFA-CC-tech] DigestMethod, DigestLocation and Dig	Jan 11, 13 2:23:33 PM	1	75.61 KB

Figure 8-2. Collection of email messages

> There is no requirement that documents in a collection have an implicit relationship or even a similarity; however, showing differentiating characteristics of related documents can be helpful for document navigation.

The Collection Dictionary

The contents of a collection are the files listed in the EmbeddedFiles. Any file in the name tree will be part of the collection, while any embedded files that are not in the tree will not. To make these files be a collection instead of just a loose set of embedded files, there needs to be a collection dictionary in the PDF that is the value of the Collection key in the document's catalog dictionary (see Example 8-6 for a simple example). Although none of the keys in the collection dictionary are required, a useful collection dictionary would contain at least two keys: D and View.

D

The D key has a string value that is the name of a PDF in the EmbeddedFiles name tree that you want the PDF viewer to show initially. It is recommended that this either be the key document in the collection or instructions about how to navigate the collection.

View

The View key has a value (of type name) that will tell the PDF viewer whether to present the list of files from the collection in details mode (D), tile mode (T), or initially hidden (H).

Example 8-6. A simple collection dictionary

```
43 0 obj
<<
    /Type /Catalog
    /Collection 44 0 R
    /Names 42 0 R        % this would be a standard EmbeddedFiles name tree
```

```
    /Pages 39 0 R        % this would be a standard page dictionary
>>
endobj

44 0 obj
<<
    /Type /Collection
    /D (Index)
    /View /D
>>
endobj
```

Collection Schema

While a simple list can be useful, it is more likely that there is additional information about each file that could be displayed as part of the collection interface presented by the PDF viewer. For example, if the files represented a movie catalog, displaying the movies' release dates and durations, as in Figure 8-3, might be useful.

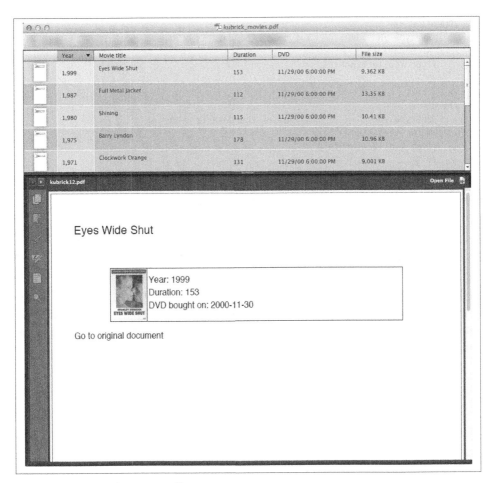

Figure 8-3. Example movie collection

To create a set of fields such as those in the example image, a collection schema dictionary is included in the collection dictionary as the value of the Schema key, with each key in the dictionary having a value that is a collection field dictionary. It would look something like Example 8-7.

Example 8-7. Example collection schema

```
<<
    /Type /CollectionSchema
    /YEAR <<
        /Subtype /N          % type of the data is a name
        /N (Year)
        /Type /CollectionField
        /O 0
    >>
```

```
    /DURATION <<
        /Subtype /N          % type of the data is a name
        /N (Duration)
        /Type /CollectionField
        /O 2
    >>
    /TITLE <<
        /Subtype /S          % type of the data is a string
        /N (Movie title)
        /Type /CollectionField
        /O 1
    >>
    /DVD <<
        /Subtype /D          % type of the data is a date
        /N (DVD)
        /Type /CollectionField
        /O 3
    >>
>>
```

In the example schema there are four fields—YEAR, DURATION, TITLE, and DVD—representing not only the names of the fields, but also their types. These fields will then be associated with each of the files specified in the EmbeddedFiles name tree through the addition of a CI key in each file specification dictionary.

 In our example, the names are in all capital letters, but that's not required in any way. Using all caps just ensures that the values will be unique names in the PDF. Example 8-8 shows a sample file specification.

Example 8-8. File specification with associated collection item dictionary

```
<<
    /F (kubrick12.pdf)
    /CI
        <<
            /Type /CollectionItem
            /YEAR 1999
            /DURATION 153
            /TITLE (Eyes Wide Shut)
            /DVD (D:20001130000000+01'00')
        >>
    /EF
        <<
            /F 35 0 R
            /UF 35 0 R
        >>
    /UF (kubrick12.pdf)
    /Type /Filespec
```

```
    /Desc (Eyes Wide Shut)
>>
```

With all that data at our disposal, we can also choose to have the file list sorted based on any of the elements of the schema rather than the default order of the Embedded Files name tree. This is done by including a Sort key in the collection dictionary whose value is its associated collection sort dictionary, as shown in Example 8-9.

Example 8-9. Example collection sort dictionary

```
% Sort the collection based on the YEAR field, in descending order
<<
    /Type /CollectionSort
    /S /YEAR
    /A false
>>
```

GoToE Actions

Previously, in "Actions" on page 79, you learned about actions that allowed a user to navigate within the existing document (GoTo), or to an external document (GoToR). Now that you've seen how to embed documents inside of a PDF, let's see how to navigate to an embedded document.

The GoToE (or "embedded go-to") action is quite similar to a remote go-to action, but it allows jumping to an embedded PDF file. Both file attachment annotations and entries in the EmbeddedFiles name tree are supported. These embedded files may in turn contain embedded files, and the GoToE action can point through one or more parent PDFs to the final destination PDF (also called the *target PDF*) via the target dictionary.

The action dictionary for a GoToE action will consist of the same three keys found in both the GoTo and GoToR actions—Type (with a value of Action), S (with a value of GoToE), and D (whose value is the destination in the target PDF).

The value of the T key in the action dictionary is a target dictionary that locates the target in relation to the source, in much the same way that a relative path describes the physical relationship between two files in a filesystem. Target dictionaries may be nested recursively to specify one or more intermediate targets before reaching the final one.

The "relative path" described by the target dictionary need not only go down the hierarchy, but may also go up, just as the ".." entry would signify in a DOS or Unix path. The "direction" is specified by the R (relationship) key and has a value of either P (parent) or C (child). Example 8-10 shows a few sample GoToE actions.

Example 8-10. Example GoToE actions

```
% Simple target of just a single embedded file
1 0 obj
```

```
<<
    /Type /Action
    /S    /GoToE
    /D    [ 0 /FitH 794 ]
    /T <<
        /N (Our First PDF.pdf)
        /R /C
    >>
>>

% Target that navigates up and then back down into another PDF
1 0 obj
<<
    /Type /Action
    /S    /GoToE
    /D    [ 0 /FitW 612 ]
    /T <<
        /R /P                   % navigate up to the parent
        /T <<
            /R /C               % now down to one of its children
            /N (Target.pdf)     % named Target.pdf
        >>
    >>
>>

% Target that navigates up twice and then back down twice
1 0 obj
<<
    /Type /Action
    /S    /GoToE
    /D    [ 0 /Fit ]
    /T <<
        /R /P                       % navigate up to the parent
        /T <<
            /R /P                   % and up again
            /T <<
                /R /C               % now down to one of its children
                /N (Intermediate.pdf) % named Intermediate.pdf
                /T <<
                    /R /C           % and one of its children
                    /N (Final.pdf)  % named Final.pdf
                >>
            >>
        >>
    >>
>>
```

What's Next

In this chapter, you learned about how to embed a file into a PDF (connecting it either to the document as a whole or to a specific place on a page) using a file specification dictionary and its associated embedded file stream. You aso learned how to instruct a PDF viewer to show your embedded files as rich collection of documents.

Next, you will learn how to work with multimedia objects in PDF, such as videos and sounds.

CHAPTER 9

Multimedia and 3D

Throughout PDF's 20 years of existence, the world of multimedia has moved from simple sounds and animations to today's interactive experiences in both 2D and 3D. PDF supports a variety of ways in which to incorporate these various types of media. This chapter will go into detail on the series of annotation types that enable the inclusion of multimedia and 3D content in PDF.

Simple Media

PDF 1.2 introduced the *sound* and *movie* annotation types, which moved PDF beyond its original vision of "static 2D electronic paper" into the fully fledged rich document format that it is today.

Sound Annotations

The *sound* annotation was originally added to PDF to provide an analog to the text annotation, except that instead of a text note, it would contain sound recorded from the computer's microphone or imported from a file that would play upon the activation of the annotation.

The annotation dictionary for a *sound* annotation consists of a Subtype of *sound*, the stream of sound data as the value of the Sound key, as well as any common annotation information required (see Example 9-1). Additionally, a Name key whose value is either Speaker or Mic may be present; this declares a predefined icon to be used when an appearance stream is not present.

The stream data for the sound should be in a common, self-describing format such as AIFF, RIFF/wav, or snd/au, and the sampling rate of the data needs to be included (as the value of the R key) in the stream dictionary. Additional information about the sound data, such as number of channels or bits per sample value per channel, may also be included as keys and values in the stream dictionary.

 Although it is most common to embed the sounds, since they are usually small, this is not required. A file specification dictionary to an external file can be used instead.

Example 9-1. Example sound annotation

```
1 0 obj
<<
    /C [ 0 1 0 ]
    /Contents (Presentation about nothing)
    /F 28
    /M D:20010213120212-05'00'
    /Name (Speaker)
    /Rect [ 22 529 42 549 ]
    /Sound 2 0 R
    /Subtype /Sound
    /T (Leonard Rosenthol)
    /Type /Annot
>>
endobj

2 0 obj
<<
    /Type /Sound
    /Length 1000        % or whatever the real length is
    /Filter /FlateDecode    % compression is good
    /R      11025        % sampling rate
>>
stream
    % binary stream data of the sound would go here...
endstream
endobj
```

Because of various limitations in the sound annotation, it is considered deprecated, and while PDF viewers will continue to support it, it is no longer recommended to use this annotation type for sounds. Instead, consider using a screen annotation (see "Screen Annotation" on page 141).

Sound actions

A sound doesn't always have to be associated with an annotation. Sometimes the sound may be played as part of a user's interaction with the PDF. A Sound action is provided for this case. As with other actions, the S key provides the type of action—Sound, in this case. The other required key in the action dictionary, as with the sound annotation, is Sound, whose value is the same data stream and associated dictionary as for the annotation. It is also possible to specify whether to play the sound synchronously or asynchronously (Synchronous) and whether to repeat it (Repeat). A sample Sound action is shown in Example 9-2.

Example 9-2. An example sound action

```
1 0 obj
<<
    /S Sound
    /Sound 2 0 R
>>
endobj

2 0 obj
<<
    /B 16
    /C 2
    /E /Signed
    /Filter /FlateDecode
    /Length 1281270
    /R 44100
    /Type /Sound
>>
stream
    % lots of stream data
endstream
endobj
```

Movie Annotations

A movie annotation enables the playing of common video or animation formats, which may also include sound or audio. The supported formats are undefined by PDF and thus left up to the viewer to choose.

To define an annotation dictionary for a movie annotation, only two keys are required: a Subtype key with the value of Movie and a Movie whose value is a movie dictionary. Additionally, an A key may be present whose value is a movie activation dictionary.

The movie dictionary

The movie dictionary defines the actual movie to be played through the use of a file specification dictionary, thus enabling the data to be either embedded or referenced externally. In addition, the aspect ratio of the movie can be provided when the annotation's Rect has been scaled but you want the movie played at a specific aspect ratio. It is also possible to provide a predefined Poster for the movie, which is a standard image XObject to be displayed on the page.

The movie activation dictionary

This dictionary provides the PDF viewer with some information about the visual presentation of the movie. To play the movie in its own floating window instead of directly on the page, provide an FWScale key along with array of scaling factors (such as [1 1] for a 100% scale). To show controls for the user to adjust the playing of the movie, provide a ShowControls key with a value of true.

The other type of information that can be provided in this dictionary is about how to play the video (or at least start playing it), including the Rate and Volume and whether to play it just once or repeat it (Mode). An example movie annotation is shown in Figure 9-1.

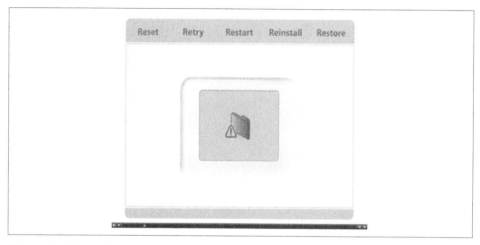

Figure 9-1. Example movie annotation

```
1 0 obj
<<
    /A << /ShowControls true >>
    /Movie <<
        /Aspect [ 308 210 ]
        /F <<
            /F (SampleMovie.mov)     % simple relative file path
            /Type FileSpec
        >>
        /Poster 2 0 R
    >>
    /Border [ 0 0 1 ]
    /C [ 1 1 1 ]
    /F 1
    /Rect [ 95.062149 496.936981 258.025818 608.048584 ]
    /Subtype /Movie
    /T (iPod Support)
```

```
    /Type /Annot
  >>
  endobj
```

Because of various limitations in the movie annotation, it is considered deprecated. While PDF viewers will continue to support it, it is no longer recommend to use this annotation type for movies. Instead, consider using a screen annotation.

Movie actions

Just as with sounds, it is also possible to invoke the playing of a movie via an action. The action is connected to a movie annotation in the same PDF, either by indirect reference through the Annotation key's value or by name via the value of the T key. The action not only allows the playing of the movie but can also specify other operations, such as Stop or Pause, via the Operation key. Example 9-3 shows a sample Movie action.

Example 9-3. Example Movie action

```
1 0 obj
<<
    /S Movie
    /T sample_iTunes.mov      % identify by name
    /Operation /Play          % not necessary, but here for example
>>
endobj
```

Multimedia

With PDF 1.5, multimedia support in PDF was brought under a single new annotation type—the screen annotation. It's called screen because its job is to define the region of the page (which will be displayed on a screen) where a media clip will be played. In fact, it doesn't actually have anything directly to do with multimedia; all of the media-specific stuff happens via the Rendition action (see "Rendition Actions" on page 142).

Screen Annotation

Although a screen annotation can be as simple as just a Subtype key with a value of Screen, it wouldn't be very useful like that. The most important part is the value of the A or AA key, where the Rendition action is specified. Also, the annotation will usually have an MK key whose value is an appearance characteristics dictionary that describes what the annotation will look like (either rendered directly or used to create the appearance stream). Example 9-4 shows a sample screen annotation.

Example 9-4. Example screen annotation

```
1 0 obj
<<
    /A 2 0 R      % the Rendition action
    /BS <<
```

```
        /S /S
        /Type /Border
        /W 1
    >>
    /MK <<
        /BC [ 0 0 1 ]
    >>
    /F 6
    /Rect [ 498.316437 702.674866 549.301331 735.843201 ]
    /Subtype /Screen
    /T (A Movie)
    /Type Annot
>>
endobj
```

The appearance characteristics dictionary

The appearance characteristics dictionary is used by screen annotations (as well as AcroForms) to describe their appearance. The values can be used to directly render the appearance, but more commonly they are used to determine the graphics to be present in the appearance stream of the annotation.

Some of the keys that may be present in this dictionary are:

R

> A multiple of 90 that represents the number of degrees of rotation for the annotation

BC

> The color to be used for the border of the annotation, described using the same array format as text color (see "Text Markup" on page 89)

BG

> The color to be used for the background of the annotation, described using the same array format as text color

Rendition Actions

The Rendition action controls the playing of multimedia content, either directly or via the use of JavaScript. It is always associated with a screen annotation; in fact, one of the required keys in the rendition action dictionary is the AN key, whose value is an indirect reference to such an annotation.

The other required keys are the action type (S), whose value is Rendition; the operation (OP) to perform (play, stop, etc.); and a rendition object as the value of the R key. Instead of the OP, a JS key could be used with a value that is the JavaScript to execute when the action is triggered. Example 9-5 shows a sample Rendition action.

Example 9-5. Example Rendition action

```
1 0 obj
<<
    /S Rendition
    /OP 0
    /R     2 0 R     % reference to rendition object
>>
endobj
```

Rendition objects

The core type of rendition is called a *media rendition*; it specifies what to play, how to play it, and where to play it. It is also possible to create an ordered list of media renditions (called a *selection rendition*) to provide the PDF viewer with options concerning the handling of media (see Figure 9-2).

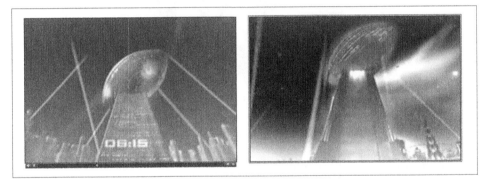

Figure 9-2. Two videos, one with and one without player controls

A rendition dictionary has only one required key, S, whose value is either MR (media rendition) or SR (selector rendition), to define what type of rendition it is. For a media rendition dictionary, it is then necessary to provide information about what to play with the (C key), how to play it (P key), and where to play it (SP key).

The value of the C key is a media clip dictionary that describes what is to be played. The media clip dictionary can specify that it is the full data for a clip or only a section, but we'll only be looking at full data here since that's the most common case by far. The data can be stored in the file (as the value of the D key) using a simple stream, or a file specification can be used for either embedded or external file references. The type of the data is declared using standard MIME types (*http://www.ietf.org/rfc/rfc2045.txt*) as the value of the CT key.

The P key's value is a media play parameters dictionary that specifies how the media is to be played. While it can specify the specific media player that is to be used (though this isn't recommend as it restricts the ability of the PDF viewer to substitute), it is more commonly used to describe whether to provide any user interface for controlling the video (C), whether or not to scale the video when playing (F), and how many times (if any) to repeat playing of the video (RC).

The remaining key element to the rendition dictionary is the SP key, whose value is a media screen parameters dictionary that describes whether to play the media on the page or in a floating window (W), as shown in Figure 9-3, and, if using a floating window, which monitor (or monitors) it can or cannot be played on (M) and at what size and location it should be played (F).

Figure 9-3. Playing video in a floating window

Example 9-6 shows a sample rendition object.

Example 9-6. Example rendition object

```
2 0 obj
<<
    /S MR
    /C <<
        /S /MCD
        /CT (video/mpeg)
        /D <<
        /F (http://www.steppublishers.com/sites/default/files/step.mov)
        /FS /URL
        /Type /Filespec
        >>
    >>
    /P <<
        /BE <<
            /C true
            /F 2
            /RC 1
        >>
    >>
```

```
    /SP <<
        /BE <<
            /W 0              % use a floating window
            /B [ 0.50 0 0 ]   % background color for the floating window
            /F <<
            /D [ 352 288 ]    % width and height of the window
                /R 0          % user cannot resize it
                /T false      % no title bar
            >>
        >>
    >>
>>
endobj
```

3D

The ability to add video or audio to a PDF file takes it beyond a static electronic document to one that is now more interactive and rich in content. Yet it remains in the realm of two dimensions. With 3D annotations, a PDF can enter the third dimension by present content that can be rotated and manipulated along all three axes (see Figure 9-4).

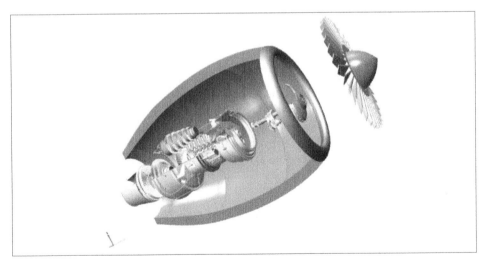

Figure 9-4. An exploded 3D view of a turbine

3D Annotations

3D artwork can be presented to the reader through the use of a 3D annotation and its 3D annotation dictionary. Additionally, a 3D annotation provides an appearance stream that has a normal (N) appearance for applications that do not support 3D annotations in addition to representing the initial display of the 3D artwork.

The 3D annotation dictionary

A 3D annotation dictionary is a standard annotation dictionary whose Subtype is 3D (see Example 9-7). In addition, it must contain a 3DD key whose value is a 3D stream that contains the 3D data as well as any additional information such as the 3D views.

 The value of 3DD can also be a 3D reference dictionary. This option is only used in the uncommon case where there are multiple annotations in the document that need to display the same 3D data.

Example 9-7. A sample 3D annotation

```
1 0 obj
<<
    /3DD 2 0 R
    /AP << /N 3 0 R >>
    /Contents (A 3D Model)
    /Rect [ 289.174988 99.371803 764.690002 493.700989 ]
    /Subtype /3D
    /Type /Annot
>>
endobj
```

3D views

When the reader presents the data in a 3D stream in a human-viewable way, it uses a series of parameters applied to the virtual camera to render it. This series of parameters, including the orientation and position of the camera and a description of the background, is called a *3D view* (or simply a *view*). These views may also specify how the 3D artwork is rendered, colored, lit, and cross-sectioned. A view can even include a list of nodes (three-dimensional areas) of the 3D artwork to make invisible.

Normally these views are dynamic, created simply by a user interactively manipulating the various parameters such as free rotation and translation (see Figure 9-5). However, it is also possible to associate a set of predefined views with the 3D artwork. For example, a mechanical drawing of a part may have specific views showing the top, bottom, left, right, front, and back of the object.

Figure 9-5. Some possible tools for a user to change the view

The various parameters for the 3D view are persisted in a *3D view dictionary*. The only key that is required in the dictionary is XN, which is the name of the view that can be presented to a user. Of the various optional parameters that can be set, the most common pair are the MS and C2W keys. The value of the C2W key is a 12-element 3D transformation matrix that specifies the position and orientation of the camera in world coordinates, while the MS key contains a value of M, which instructs the reader to use the C2W value. An example of a 3D view dictionary is shown in Example 9-8.

Example 9-8. Example view dictionary

```
<<
    /C2W [ 1.0 0.0 0.0 0.0 0.0 -1.0 0.0 1.0 0.0 0.000006 -387.131989 -0.099388 ]
    /MS /M
    /Type /3DView
    /XN (Default)
>>
```

3D streams

A *3D stream* is a stream whose contents are in either the U3D (*http://bit.ly/16Zjl5w*) or the PRC (*http://bit.ly/1aEx7NQ*) format. In addition, its associated dictionary is required to have a Subtype key whose value declares the data format (either U3D or PRC).

The 3D stream's dictionary may also contain an array of 3D views associated with the 3D artwork as the value of a VA key. The DV key is used to specify which view is the default or initial view, either as an integer index into the VA array or as a string that matches one of the names of the provided views. Example 9-9 shows an example of a 3D stream with views.

Example 9-9. Example 3D stream with views

```
1 0 obj
<<
    /Type /3D
    /Subtype /U3D
    /VA [ 2 0 R 3 0 R 4 0 R ]
    /DV 0    % the first one is the default
>>
stream
% U3D data goes here...
endstream
endobj

2 0 obj
<<
    /BG << /C [ 0.752945 0.752945 0.752945 ] /Subtype /SC >>
    /C2W [
        -0.399527 -0.916721 0.0 -0.238227
        0.103825 0.965644 -0.885226 0.385801
        -0.259869 758.682983 -202.897003 207.556000
    ]
    /CO 727.596008
    /MS M
    /Type /3DView
```

```
    /XN (Default)
>>
```

Markups on 3D

The various markup annotations that were introduced previously for normal PDF page content can also be applied to specific views of 3D artwork.

In order to specify that a given markup annotation is associated with a 3D annotation, an ExData key is added to the standard annotation dictionary whose value is a 3D markup dictionary.

A 3D markup dictionary specifies the 3D annotation and 3D view that the markup is associated with and may also include an MD5 hash of the 3D data to enable the viewer to make sure the 3D artwork hasn't changed since the annotation was applied. Figure 9-6 shows some example 3D markup.

Figure 9-6. Example 3D markup

```
% Polygon annotation
1 0 obj
<<
    /BE << /I 2.0 /S C >>
    /BS << /W 3.0 >>
    /C [ 0.0 1.0 1.0 ]
    /ExData 2 0 R
    /Rect [ 302.412994 403.898987 399.747986 520.927979 ]
    /Subtype /Polygon
    /Type /Annot
```

```
    /Vertices [
        315.097992 506.010010 364.582001 508.194000
        387.140991 423.052002 315.097992 416.502014
        315.097992 506.010010 ]
>>

% 3D markup dictionary
2 0 obj
<<
    /Type /ExData
    /Subtype /Markup3D
    /3DA 2 0 R     % this is the 3D annotation
    /3DV 3 0 R     % and this is the view
>>
```

What's Next

In this chapter, you learned about multimedia and 3D annotations. Next you will learn about how to create content and annotations that are only visible (or print) when certain criteria are met.

CHAPTER 10

Optional Content

Optional content is a feature of PDF that allows specific graphic objects and/or annotations to be visible only when a certain set of criteria is met. These criteria can be specified by the author of the content—for example, that this content should only appear on the screen and never print—or can be specified by the user via some interaction with the viewer. This feature is useful for a variety of things, ranging from CAD drawings to maps to multilanguage documents and more.

Optional Content Groups

The basic building block for defining optional content is the *optional content group* (OCG), which is a dictionary that consists of the required Type (which is always OCG), the required Name of the group (which may be displayed by a viewer), and the Usage key, which declares how the group is to be used.

Content State

A group is assigned a state, which is either ON or OFF. States may be set automatically by the viewer (based on the Usage), programmatically, or through the viewer's user interface. Content belonging to a group is visible when the group is ON and invisible when it is OFF.

Content may belong to multiple groups, which may have conflicting states.

Usage

Content is usually grouped together because it shares some common feature. It may be the language of the content, or that it is only for use on screen. The *optional content usage dictionary*, which is the value of the Usage key in the optional content group dictionary, declares the commonality (see Example 10-1). This usage information is then used by the PDF viewer to determine whether to evaluate the group's state based on external factors in conjunction with the value of the AS key in the optional content configuration dictionary (see "Optional Content Configuration" on page 155).

A Usage dictionary may contain any number of keys, if the group has multiple things in common. The most commonly used keys are the following:

Export

> The value of this key is a dictionary containing a single key, ExportState, whose value (of type Name) is either ON or OFF, declaring whether this content should be exported by the viewer into a nonoptional-content-aware format (such as raster images or Postscript).

Print

> The key's value is a dictionary containing a single key, PrintState, whose value (of type Name) is either ON or OFF declaring whether this content should be printed.

View

> The value of this key is a dictionary containing a single key, ViewState, whose value (of type Name) is either ON or OFF, declaring whether this content should be displayed on the screen (or whatever the default "view" of the viewer is).

Zoom

> The dictionary value of this key contains either the min key, the max key, or both. The values of these keys, if present, specify the minimum and maximum zoom/magnification (in percentage) at which the group should be considered ON.

Language

> The value of this key is a dictionary that declares the natural language of the content in the group via its Lang key.

 Although Language is a great way to group content, it is not automatically detected and assigned a group state by common viewers.

Example 10-1. Some example optional content groups

```
10 0 obj
<<
    /Name (Watermark)
    /Type OCG
    /Usage <<
        /Print << /PrintState /ON >>
        /View << /ViewState /OFF >>
    >>
>>
endobj

11 0 obj
<<
    /Name (Do Not Print Or Export)
    /Type OCG
    /Usage <<
        /Export << /ExportState /OFF >>
        /Print << /PrintState /OFF >>
        /View << /ViewState /ON >>
    >>
>>
endobj

12 0 obj
<<
    /Name (zoom = {0% 100%})
    /Type OCG
    /Usage <<
        /Zoom    <<
            /max 1
        >>
    >>
>>
endobj

13 0 obj
<<
    /Name (zoom = {100% 200%})
    /Type OCG
    /Usage <<
        /Zoom <<
            /max 2
            /min 1
        >>
    >>
>>
endobj
```

Optional Content Membership

While most content only needs to be a member of a single optional content group and its associated usage dictionary, sometimes content may belong to multiple groups, and those groups may have conflicting states. In order to provide the viewer with the necessary information to resolve such potential conflicts, this type of content should be associated with an *optional content membership dictionary* (OCMD) instead of an optional content group.

An OCMD is, at its heart, a list of the OCGs that specify the various potential visibility states along with either a visibility policy or a visibility expression that describes how to determine the state.

Visibility Policies

A visibility policy is the simplest way to specify how the various OCG states will be resolved (see Example 10-2). This is the preferred method and should be used in favor of visibility expressions if possible.

The policy is specified by a single name object with one of four possible values. This value is that of the P key in the OCMD. The available policy values are the following:

AllOn
> Visible only if all of the entries in the OCGs are ON

AnyOn
> Visible if any of the entries in the OCGs are ON

AnyOff
> Visible if any of the entries in the OCGs are OFF

AllOff
> Visible only if all of the entries in the OCGs are OFF

Example 10-2. Example visibility policy

```
<<
/Type /OCMD                 % Content belonging to this optional content
                            % membership dictionary is controlled by the states
/OCGs [12 0 R 13 0 R 14 0 R] % of three optional content groups.
/P /AllOn                    % Content is visible only if the state of all three
                            % groups is ON; otherwise it's hidden.
>>
```

Visibility Expressions

A visibility expression, as the name implies, allows for more complex Boolean expressions in defining how the various OCG states should be resolved. When a viewer evaluates a visibility expression, if the expression evaluates to true, then the optional content group is in the ON state. If it evaluates to false, then the state is OFF.

The expression is an array whose first element is a name representing a Boolean operator (And, Or, or Not), while subsequent elements are either optional content groups or other visibility expressions. If the first element of the expression is Not, then there is only one subsequent element; otherwise (for And or Or), it can have one or more subsequent elements.

 It might seem strange that an And or Or expression could have only a single associated element, but that element can itself be a visibility expression instead of a reference to an OCG.

Example 10-3 shows what the visibility policy would look like as a visibility expression.

Example 10-3. Simple visibility expression

```
<<
    /Type /OCMD
    /VE [/And 12 0 R 13 0 R 14 0 R]
>>
```

Example 10-4 shows a more complex expression that relates five different groups, represented by the objects 1 through 5 in the PDF, named OCG 1 through OCG 5, respectively. If written out, the example would read as "OCG 1"; OR (NOT "OCG 2") OR ("OCG 3" AND "OCG 4" AND "OCG 5")".

Example 10-4. Complex visibility expression

```
<<
    /Type /OCMD
    /VE [/Or                        % Visibility expression: OR
        1 0 R                       % OCG 1
        [/Not 2 0 R]                % NOT OCG 2
        [/And 3 0 R 4 0 R 5 0 R]    % OCG 3 AND OCG 4 AND OCG 5
    ]
>>
```

Optional Content Configuration

An *optional content configuration dictionary* (OCCD) represents a preset configuration of the state for one or more groups. A PDF (that has OCGs) may contain several OCCDs, but must include at least one. The reason for the one is that when a document is first opened by a conforming reader, the groups' states are initialized based on the document's default OCCD.

The default OCCD is specified as the value of the D key in the optional content properties dictionary, which is itself referenced from the document catalog dictionary (see "Optional Content Membership" on page 154 and "The Catalog Dictionary" on page 21).

While all of the keys in the OCCD are optional, it is most common to have at least some combination of BaseState and ON or OFF present. BaseState is a name (either ON, OFF, or Unchanged) that represents the state of all groups to start with. This "base state" can then be adjusted through the use of the ON and/or OFF keys, which list specific OCGs whose state to set to ON or OFF. It is also common to give the OCCD a name via the Name key. Example 10-5 shows a simple optional content configuration dictionary.

Example 10-5. Simple OCCD

```
2 0 obj
<<
    /Name     (Example)
    /BaseState    /ON      % turn them all on
    /OFF [ 1 0 R ]         % except this one
>>
endobj
```

Order Key

In some cases, the choices about which content should be visible and which should not are made by the author of the content and remain stable throughout the content's life. However, most content that is described with optional content groups is done so that a user can manually change the visibility of the content. For example, with a complex architectural or electrical diagram, the user may need to turn on or off various groups of graphic elements in order to see just the important ones.

To request that a PDF viewer present a list of user-configurable optional content to the user, the Order key is used. For a simple list of groups like the one in Figure 10-1, the value of the key is a one-dimensional array of OCGs.

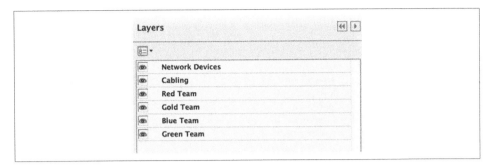

Figure 10-1. A simple list of optional content groups

```
% Present 6 OCGs in the list of OCGs
<<
    /Order[
        40 0 R 42 0 R 38 0 R 32 0 R 36 0 R 34 0 R
    ]
>>
```

It is also possible to group the OCGs in various hierarchical groupings, in a way that might be helpful to the user or that just generally represents logical groupings of the content. For example, if there is a specialized subcategory of elements, they can be collected together.

The name of the group can be taken from the OCG that immediately precedes the subarray of elements, or it can be specified by a text string in the subarray. Figure 10-2 shows a few examples of hierarchical groupings of OCGs.

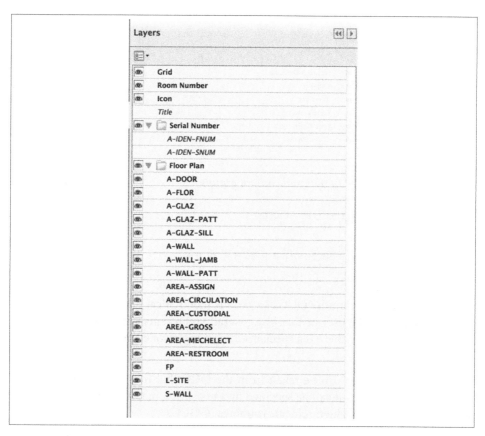

Figure 10-2. Examples of hierarchical lists of optional content groups

```
% Using the Name of an OCG for the name of the group
<<
    /Order[
        24 0 R 37 0 R 34 0 R 25 0 R
        30 0 R [
            32 0 R 31 0 R
        ]
        22 0 R [
            27 0 R 28 0 R 29 0 R 36 0 R 40 0 R 23 0 R 26 0 R 35 0 R 41
            0 R 43 0 R 45 0 R 44 0 R 46 0 R 42 0 R 38 0 R 33 0 R 39 0 R
        ]
    ]
>>

% Using a text string for the name of the group
<<
    /Order [
        [(Group 1) 1 0 R 2 0 R]
        [(Group 2) 3 0 R 4 0 R]
```

```
        ]
>>
```

RBGroups

The OCGs that are listed in the array value of the Order key are simply presented as a (possibly hierarchical) list. Users can turn them on and off in any combination that they wish. For many use cases, such as architectural or electronical diagrams, this works well. If you were using optional content groups to allow the user to select a language for the content of the document, for example, it would not make sense to have text in multiple languages showing at the same time (with one version on top of another!). To apply the logic that only one of a group of items can be "on" at a time in the user interface of a view, the RBGroups key is used.

The *RB* in RBGroups stands for radio button.

The value of the RBGroups key is an array of one or more arrays, where each one represents the collection of OCGs whose states should be grouped together using the radio button metaphor—just one at a time. Figure 10-3 illustrates the use of RBGroups.

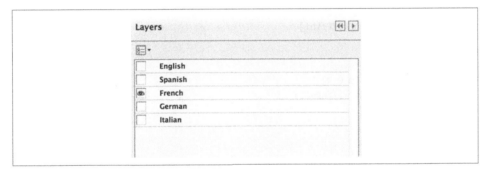

Figure 10-3. RBGroups example

```
<<
    /RBGroups [
        [ 55 0 R 57 0 R 59 0 R 61 0 R 63 0 R ]
    ]
>>
```

It is also possible to use complex visibility expressions to accomplish the same thing, but RBGroups are easier and more compatible with various viewers; therefore, they are more common and preferred.

AS (Automatic State)

The automatic state (AS) key in the OCCD declares which of the available usage values are to be checked by the PDF viewer and used to automatically adjust the state of various OCGs as illustrated in Example 10-6. The value of the AS key is an array of usage application dictionaries, each one stating which OCGs are to be checked for which type of event (or situation) and the category of usage.

Example 10-6. Example OCCD with automatic state

```
<<
    /Order[17 0 R]
    /ON[17 0 R 36 0 R]
    /AS [
            <<
                /Event/View
                /OCGs[36 0 R]
                /Category[/View]
            >>
            <<
                /Event/Print
                /OCGs[37 0 R]
                /Category[/Print]
            >>
            <<
                /Event/Export
                /OCGs[38 0 R]
                /Category[/Export]
            >>
    ]
>>
endobj
```

Optional Content Properties

Even after all the OCGs, OCMDs, and OOCDs are added to the PDF, there is still one more dictionary that is required. This is the *optional content properties dictionary*; it is the value of the OCProperties key in the document catalog dictionary. Without this, a viewer will not be aware that there is any optional content in the PDF.

There are two required keys in the properties dictionary:

OCGs

> This is an array of every single OCG in the PDF, regardless of how it is used, listed in any order. If it is not listed in this array, then the viewer can choose to ignore it when it is encountered later.

D

> The value of this key is the default optional content configuration dictionary for the PDF.

Optionally, if the PDF contains multiple OCCDs, they can be listed as the value of the Configs key in this dictionary. A sample optional content properties dictionary is shown in Example 10-7.

Example 10-7. Example OCProperties dictionary

```
<<
    /OCGs    [ 1 0 R 2 0 R 3 0 R ]    % we have 3 OCGs in this PDF
    /D    <<
        /BaseState    /ON             % and they are all on
    >>
>>
```

Marking Content as Optional

So far in this chapter we've seen how to create optional content groups and all of the infrastructure for making them available to a PDF viewer and its users. However, a PDF containing all of the previously described objects is still missing one key component—how are the content elements connected to the optional content groups or optional content membership dictionaries that may affect their visibility? Any content whose visibility will be affected by a given optional content group is said to *belong to* (or have membership in) that group.

Optional Content in Content Streams

To specify which specific content elements of a content stream are to be associated with an optional content group or optional content membership dictionary, they need to be enclosed between the marked content operators BDC and EMC. The BDC operator will use the tag of OC, and the associated property list specifies the OCG or OCMD to which the content belongs. Since the reference to the group is via its indirect object, the property list must used the named resource form for property lists.

Example 10-8 shows a simple example of how to mark content in a stream as optional.

Example 10-8. Simple optional content example

```
% (partial/incomplete) page object
18 0 obj
<<
```

```
    /Type /Page
    /Contents 19 0 obj
    /CropBox [ 0 0 612 792 ]
    /MediaBox [ 0 0 612 792 ]
    /Resources <<
    /Properties << /MC0 20 0 R >>
        >>
>>
endobj

% (partial/incomplete) content stream object
19 0 obj
<<>>
stream
/OC /MC0 BDC      % this group is part of the MC0 OCG
    0 g
    1 i
    BT
        /T1_0 1 Tf
        12 0 0 12 234 364 Tm
        (This page intentionally blank\000)Tj
    ET
EMC
endstream
endobj

% optional content group
20 0 obj
<<
    /Intent /View
    /Name (Alternate Content)
    /Type /OCG
>>
endobj
```

Content can be associated with one or more OCGs and/or OCMDs, and the content of a group need not be contiguous in the content stream, or even in the same content stream (see Figure 10-4). This makes optional content extremely flexible for many purposes (see Figure 10-5).

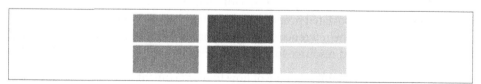

Figure 10-4. Multiple uses of the same group

```
    % Content stream with each color in a separate OCG
```

```
/OC /MC0 BDC        % Red rectangles
1 0 0 rg
279 159.356 -211 86 re
f
EMC

/OC /MC1 BDC        % Green rectangles
0 1 0 rg
755 160.356 -211 86 re
f
EMC

/OC /MC2 BDC        % Blue rectangles
0 0 1 rg
519 159.356 -211 86 re
f
EMC

/OC /MC0 BDC        % Red rectangles
1 0 0 rg
279 62.356 -211 86 re
f
EMC

/OC /MC1 BDC        % Green rectangles
0 1 0 rg
755 63.356 -211 86 re
f
EMC

/OC /MC2 BDC        % Blue rectangles
0 0 1 rg
519 62.356 -211 86 re
f
EMC
```

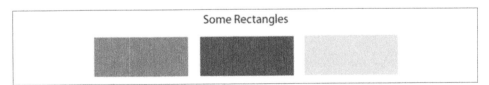

Figure 10-5. Content belonging to multiple groups

```
% Content stream

% This content doesn't belong to any group
BT
0 0 0 rg
/T1_0 1 Tf
27 0 0 27 314.2861 142.3242 Tm
```

```
        [(S)-6(ome R)-4(ec)-12.9(tangles)]TJ
        ET

    /OC /MC3 BDC          % everything here is part of MC3
        /OC /MC0 BDC      % this belongs to MC3 *AND* MC0
            1 0 0 rg
            279 159.356 -211 86 re
            f
        EMC

        /OC /MC1 BDC       % this belongs to MC3 *AND* MC1
            0 1 0 rg
            755 160.356 -211 86 re
            f
        EMC

        /OC /MC2 BDC       % this belongs to MC3 *AND* MC2
            0 0 1 rg
            519 159.356 -211 86 re
            f
        EMC
    EMC
```

Optional Content for Form XObjects

For form XObjects or image XObjects that are used only in a single content stream, simply marking up the invoking stream can be done easily. However, when such objects are used in multiple content streams and will be consistently in the same group(s), it is easier to take advantage of the OC key in the XObject dictionary. The value of the OC key in the XObject dictionary is an indirect reference to the optional content group or optional content membership dictionary to which it belongs. Example 10-9 illustrates this usage.

Example 10-9. Example form XObject with associated OCG

```
35 0 obj
<<
    /FormType 1
    /Subtype/Form
    /Length 91
    /Matrix[1.0 0.0 0.0 1.0 0.0 0.0]
    /BBox[0.0 -31.7999 79.9918 0.143921]
    /Resources<</Font<</TT0 32 0 R>>>>
    /OC 37 0 R
>>
stream
0 0.75 1 rg
0 i
BT
/TT0 1 Tf
0 Tc 0 Tw 0  Ts 100  Tz 0 Tr
```

```
24 0 0 24 0 -24 Tm
(DRAFT)Tj
ET

endstream
endobj
```

If a form XObject or image XObject has an OC key and the same XObject is also part of an optional content group or optional content membership dictionary configured inside of a content stream, the combination of the two states (treated as an AND) will be used to determine the visibility of the object. For example, if the OCG value of the OC key evaluates to ON but the content stream evaluates to OFF, then the state for the object will be OFF.

It is also possible to have individual content of a form XObject be part of an OCG or OCMD. In that instance, the visibility of the XObject will be evaluated, and if its state is ON, the specific graphics objects will be evaluated.

Optional Content for Annotations

Although the individual content elements of the appearance stream of an annotation can be marked up and associated with specific optional content groups or optional content membership dictionaries, it is more common to simply associate the entire annotation. This not only hides the annotation from view, but also ensures that a PDF viewer will not provide any user interaction with the element. This is quite useful for interactive forms, as a way to hide or show elements based on other criteria (see Chapter 7).

As with form or image XObjects, the value of the OC key in the annotation dictionary is an indirect reference to the optional content group or optional content membership dictionary to which it belongs. Example 10-10 demonstrates.

Example 10-10. Example annotation with associated OCG

```
20 0 obj
<<
    /Type         /Annot
    /Subtype      /Highlight
    /Rect         [ 252.594 593.733 322.077 623.211 ]
    /C       [ 1 1 0 ]
    /OC 37 0 R
>>
```

What's Next

In this chapter you learned about optional content groups, including how to create them and associate content with them. Next you will look at how to add semantic richness to PDF content.

CHAPTER 11

Tagging and Structure

Structured PDF

As you've seen in all the previous chapters, PDF provides the ability to draw text, vectors, raster images, and even video and 3D onto a page that can be displayed or printed. However, the content is just that: a series of drawing instructions. It has no semantic or structural context. There is nothing that delineates one paragraph from another or one image from another. In fact, there isn't even a concept of a paragraph or a word—just a bunch of glyphs and their associated encoding.

This limitation is addressed by a feature of PDF called *logical structure*. It enables associating a hierarchical grouping of objects, called *structure elements*, with the various graphic objects on the page and any additional attributes needed to sufficiently describe those objects. This is quite similar in concept to markup languages such as HTML or XML, but in PDF that structure and content are in separate logical areas of the PDF rather than being intermixed (as they are in HTML, for example). This separation allows the ordering and nesting of logical elements to be entirely independent of the order and location of graphic objects on the document's pages.

While there is a series of predefined types of structure elements that enable the organization of a document into chapters and sections or the identification of special elements such as figures, tables, and footnotes, the facilities provided by PDF are quite extensible. This extensibility allows writers to choose what structural information to include and how to represent it, while enabling processors to navigate the file without knowing the specific structural conventions.

Figure 11-1. Structure tree for a simple page

Figure 11-2. The page created from the above structure tree

The Structure Tree

As previously mentioned, the structural elements are arranged in a hierarchical structure called the StructTree, or *structure tree*. At the root of the tree is the *structure tree root*, a dictionary whose Type key has a value of StructTreeRoot (see Example 11-1). There are two other things that are required to be present in the root: the first of the children in the tree and a grouping of structure elements by page (see Figure 11-1 and its result, Figure 11-2).

The K key in the root points to the first structural element in the structure tree. Its value can either be a single structure element dictionary or an array of structure element dictionaries. Most tagged PDFs will have a single entry, which is a structure element of type Document.

The ParentTree key is a number tree that groups all structural elements on a page together with an associated number/index. While it is more logical to have the ordinal page number represent the number/index in the number tree, that is not required, as we will see when we learn how to associate structure with a page (in "Associating Structure to Content" on page 174).

Example 11-1. Example structure tree root

```
1 0 obj
<<
    /K 3 0 R                % the first structure element
    /ParentTree 2 0 R       % number tree of the elements
    /Type /StructTreeRoot
>>
endobj

2 0 obj
<<
    % a one-page document with two elements on it
    /Nums [ 0 [4 0 R 5 0 R] ]
>>
endobj
```

Structure Elements

Each structural element is represented by a dictionary whose Type key has a value of StructElem. The specific type of structural element that it represents is specified as the value of the S key. That value is a name object and can be anything, though it is recommended to stick to the values discussed in "Standard structure types" on page 170.

> If you choose to use your own name for a structure element, be sure to use a role map (see "Role Mapping" on page 172) to map it to the closest standard structure type.

The P key in the structure element dictionary has as its value the parent element in the tree, so that it is possible for a processor to navigate the tree in all directions. In the case of the first child, the parent will be the StructTreeRoot.

As with the *StructTreeRoot*, the children of each element can be found as the value of the K key. The value of K can be a structure element, an array of structure elements, or an integer that represents the marked content ID (MCID) on the target page for the content. In addition, it is possible to have a reference to an annotation or an XObject if you are referring to the entire object as the content of that particular structure element.

> While it is possible to have a direct reference to an XObject, it is more common to simply include the XObject inside of a marked content sequence (see "Marked Content Operators" on page 46).

Although it's not required, it is common to have a `Pg` key present in the structure element's dictionary whose value is the page dictionary where the content representing the element is displayed.

One other common key in the structure element's dictionary is the `Lang` key, which can be used to clearly identify the natural language applicable to a given structure element (and its children, unless otherwise overridden). The value of this key is a standard RFC 3066 (*http://www.ietf.org/rfc/rfc3066.txt*) code. Example 11-2 demonstrates a few sample structure elements.

Example 11-2. Example structure elements

```
2 0 obj
<<
    /K [ 3 0 R 4 0 R ]    % there are two children to the document
    /Lang (en-US)
    /P 1 0 R              % back to the struct root
    /S /Document
    /Type /StructElem
>>
endobj

3 0 obj
<<
    /K 0         % this is MCID 0 on the page
    /P 2 0 R
    /Pg 5 0 R    % and here is the page
    /S /P        % P(aragraph)
    /Type /StructElem
>>
endobj

4 0 obj
<<
    /K 1         % MCID 1
    /P 2 0 R
    /Pg 5 0 R    % and here is the page
    /S /Figure
    /Type /StructElem
>>
endobj
```

Standard structure types

By defining a standard for the types—that is, the value of the S key in a structure element dictionary—PDF provides for a common vocabulary that PDF writers can use to ensure that processors are able to understand the incorporated semantics. These types are categorized into *grouping elements*, *block-level structural elements* (BLSEs), and *inline-level structural elements* (ILSEs), depending on whether the element refers to actual content and how that content would normally be laid out on a page.

Grouping elements

Grouping elements have no presentation concepts, but serve strictly to group other sets of elements together. Document, for example, will be the single root structural element for most PDFs. Other common grouping elements are similar to those found in other markup systems, such as Sect, Div, and BlockQuote.

Block-level structural elements

A block-level structure element is any region of text or other content that is laid out in the block progression direction, such as a paragraph, heading, list item, or footnote. Table 11-1 lists some of these types of content and their related structure elements.

Table 11-1. BLSEs and related structure elements

Structure type	Description
H	(Heading) A label for a subdivision of a document's content.
H1–H6	Headings with specific levels.
P	(Paragraph) A low-level division of text.
L	(List) A sequence of items of like meaning and importance. Its immediate children will be list items (LI).
LI	(List item) An individual member of a list.
Lbl	(Label) A name or number that distinguishes a given item from others in the same list or other group of like items. For example, in a dictionary list, it contains the term being defined; in a bulleted or numbered list, it contains the bullet character or the number of the list item and any associated punctuation.
LBody	(List body) The descriptive content of a list item. For example, in a dictionary list, it contains the definition of the term.
Table	(Table) A two-dimensional layout of rectangular data cells, possibly having a complex substructure. It contains either one or more table rows (TR) or an optional table head (THead) followed by one or more table body elements (TBody) and an optional table footer (TFoot).
TR	(Table row) A row of headings or data in a table.
TH	(Table header cell) A table cell containing header text describing one or more rows or columns of the table.
TD	(Table data cell) A table cell containing data that is part of the table's content.
THead	(Table header row group) A group of rows that constitute the header of a table.
TBody	(Table body row group) A group of rows that constitute the main body portion of a table.
TFoot	(Table footer row group) A group of rows that constitute the footer of a table.

All other standard structure types will either be treated as ILSEs or appear as artifacts (see "Artifacts" on page 172).

Inline-level structural elements

An inline-level structural element contains a portion of text or other content having specific styling characteristics or playing a specific role in the document. Within the containing BLSE, consecutive ILSEs (possibly intermixed with other content items) are considered to be laid out consecutively in the inline-progression direction (e.g., left to right in Western writing systems). An ILSE may also contain a BLSE. Table 11-2 lists some common types of inline-level structural elements.

Table 11-2. ILSEs

Structure type	Description
Span	(Span) A generic inline portion of text having no particular inherent characteristics.
Quote	(Quotation) An inline portion of text attributed to someone other than the author of the surrounding text.
Note	(Note) An item of explanatory text, such as a footnote or an endnote, that is referred to from within the body of the document.
Reference	(Reference) A citation to content elsewhere in the document.
BibEntry	(Bibliography entry) A reference identifying the external source of some cited content.
Code	(Code) A fragment of computer program text.
Link	(Link) An association between a portion of the ILSE's content and a corresponding link annotation.
Annot	(Annotation) An association between a portion of the ILSE's content and a corresponding annotation.

Additional structure elements can be found in ISO 32000-1:2008, 14.8.

Artifacts

Artifacts are graphic objects that are added by the authoring system but don't necessarily represent the author's original content, such as page or Bates numbers or background images. Graphic objects that aren't necessary to understand the author's content, such as repeating headers or footnote rules, are also identified as artifacts.

An artifact is distinguished from real content by enclosing it in a marked content sequence with the tag `Artifact`. An example is shown in Example 11-3.

Example 11-3. Example page number artifact

```
% a part of a content stream

/Artifact
BMC
    (Page 1) Tj
EMC
```

Role Mapping

When using custom values for a structure type, it is important to provide a role map dictionary to describe which of the standard structure types it most closely resembles. The role map dictionary is simply a list of keys corresponding to the custom types in use for each key, the value is the name of the standard structure type. This dictionary is specified as the value of the `RoleMap` key in the structure tree root. An example of `RoleMap` is shown in Example 11-4.

Example 11-4. Example of a RoleMap

```
1 0 obj
<<
    /K 3 0 R                 % the first structure element
    /ParentTree 2 0 R        % number tree of the elements
    /Type /StructTreeRoot
    /RoleMap 6 0 R           % map the custom elements
>>
endobj

2 0 obj
<<
    % a one-page document with two elements on it
    /Nums [ 0 [4 0 R 5 0 R] ]
>>
endobj

3 0 obj
<<
    /K [ 4 0 R 5 0 R ]       % there are two children to the document
    /Lang (en-US)
    /P 1 0 R                 % back to the struct root
    /S /Document
    /Type /StructElem
>>
endobj

4 0 obj
<<
    /K 0                     % this is MCID 0 on the page
    /P 3 0 R
    /Pg 10 0 R               % and here is the page
    /S /Para                 % Para(graph)
    /Type /StructElem
>>
endobj

5 0 obj
<<
    /K 1                     % MCID 1
    /P 3 0 R
    /Pg 10 0 R               % and here is the page
    /S /Chap                 % Chap(ter)
    /Type /StructElem
>>
endobj

6 0 obj
<<
    /Para     /P
    /Chap     /Sect
```

```
    >>
endobj
```

Associating Structure to Content

Identifying which graphics operators in a content steam are associated with a specific structure element is done by simply enclosing those elements in a pair of marked content operators—specifically BDC and EMC—and an associated property list. A simple example is presented in Example 11-5.

Example 11-5. Simple marked content example

```
BT
    /TT0 1 Tf
    -0.018 Tw 60 0 0 60 158.1533 714.3984 Tm
    /P <</MCID 0 >>BDC
        [(Hello W)80.2(orld)]TJ
    EMC
ET

/Figure <</MCID 1 >>BDC
    q
    541 0 0 407 36 189.4000244 cm
    /Im0 Do
    Q
EMC
```

This content refers to the structure elements from Example 11-2, which consisted of two numbered elements, 0 and 1, the numbers that are referenced by the MCID keys in the property lists.

 Although the name used in this example for the tag around the image is Figure, it could have been Foo or any other string. It is the value of the S key in the structure element dictionary that actually determines the structure type. Using the same name is a very good idea and is highly recommended!

Although applying structure to the graphics operators in the page's content stream is the most common approach, it is also possible to apply structure inside other types of content streams, such as the one associated with a form XObject. In most cases, the entire form XObject represents a complete structure element and you can just enclose the Do operator inside of the marked content, as in the preceeding example. However, it is also possible to apply the same type of marked content operators to individual graphics operators inside of the XObject's content stream.

When applying marked content operators to the individual graphics operators inside of the XObject's content stream, it is not permitted to also include a Do for that XObject inside of some other structure element.

Tagged PDFs

Although adding structure to a PDF can be quite useful, there are additional rules that can be applied during the writing of the PDF content to enable an even richer set of semantics in the final PDF. When these rules are applied, the PDF is called a *tagged PDF*.

A tagged PDF document conforms to the following rules:

- All text shall be represented in a form that can be converted to Unicode.
- Word breaks shall be represented explicitly.
- Actual content shall be distinguished from artifacts of layout and pagination.
- Content shall be given in an order related to its appearance on the page, as determined by the PDF writer.
- A basic layout model for describing the arrangement of structure elements on the page shall be applied.
- The set of standard structure types shall be used to define the meaning of structure elements.

One of the most important purposes of these rules is to ensure that all of the text in the page content can be determined reliably.

A tagged PDF document will also contain a *mark information dictionary* with a value of true for the Marked key. The mark information dictionary is the value of the MarkInfo key in the document catalog dictionary.

There is a typo in ISO 32000-1, 14.7.1, where the key is referred to as the Marking key instead of Marked. Don't be confused—it's Marked.

What's Next

In this chapter, you learned about how to add semantic richness to your PDF content through tagging and structure. Next you will see how to incorporate metadata into a PDF at the document as well as the object level.

CHAPTER 12

Metadata

This chapter will explore the various ways in which metadata can be incorporated into a PDF file, from the simplest document-level strings to rich XML attached to individual objects.

The Document Information Dictionary

It was clear even with the original 1.0 version of PDF that the presence of metadata was a requirement for any file format, and certainly one that would be representing documents for electronic distribution and storage. For this purpose, the *document information dictionary* (or info dictionary, or even just info dict) was created (see Example 12-1).

As the name implies, the info dictionary is a standard PDF dictionary object. However, unlike every other object you've encountered so far, this object is referenced not from the catalog, but instead from the trailer. The original PDF 1.0 specification documented four (optional) keys for this dictionary, each one allowing only a string value encoded in PDFDocEncoding.

Author
  The name of the person(s) who created the document.

CreationDate
  The date and time the document was created, formatted as a date.

 Dates, as a type of string, were added to PDF in version 1.1, so very early PDF files may have the value of this key as a simple string.

Creator

The software used to author the original document that was used as the basis for conversion to PDF. If the PDF was created directly, the value may be left blank or may be the same as the `Producer`.

Producer

The name of the product that created the PDF.

In PDF 1.1, four additional (optional) keys were added, each allowing a string value encoded in PDFDocEncoding:

Title

The document's title.

Subject

The document's subject.

Keywords

Any keywords associated with this document.

ModDate

The date and time the document was most recently modified, formatted as a date.

While the PDF specification documented only those eight keys, developers and users were originally free to add additional keys to the dictionary whose values could be of any type. Later, the PDF specification (and now ISO 32000-1 itself) restricted the values to only those of type text string (see "String Objects" on page 4).

 Since ISO 32000-1 allows only for values of type text string, developers cannot store more complex information in a dictionary or a stream.

Example 12-1. Example info dictionary

```
1 0 obj
<<
    /Title (PostScript Language Reference, Third Edition)
    /Author (Adobe Systems Incorporated)
    /Creator (Adobe FrameMaker 5.5.3 for Power Macintosh®)
    /Producer (Acrobat Distiller 3.01 for Power Macintosh)
    /CreationDate (D:19970915110347-08'00')
    /ModDate (D:19990209153925-08'00')
    /DEV1_CustomKey (Here is a sample custom key using a proper second class name)
    /CustomKey2 (Here is a sample custom key improperly using a first class name)
>>
endobj
```

Metadata Streams

As you can see, the info dictionary has a number of limitations, including data typing and handling of complex structures (such as arrays or dictionaries), not to mention being associated with only the document as a whole and not individual objects in the PDF.

To address these concerns, a new type of metadata was introduced called a *metadata stream* (because, as you can probably guess, it's stored as a stream object). These streams can be associated not only with the document but with any object in it (though some are more likely to have them than others). As these are streams, they can have any of the standard compression or encoding filters applied to the data. However, it is strongly recommended that at least the document-level metadata stream be stored in plain text. In fact, some of the PDF standards specifically require that the document-level metadata stream be stored in plain text (see Chapter 13).

 Although the reason for recommending plain-text metadata streams is to enable non-PDF-aware tools to examine, catalog, and classify documents, it turns out that doing so may actually be problematic if incremental updates are made to the document. When the document is updated, there will be a second (updated) metadata stream, which will confuse a non-PDF-aware tool.

The contents of a metadata stream are in a specific Extensible Markup Language (XML) grammar known as the Extensible Metadata Platform (XMP), which has been standardized as ISO 16684-1.

XMP

In XMP, metadata consists of a set of properties. Properties are always associated with a particular entity (referred to as a *resource*). That is, the properties are "about" the resource. Any given property has a name and a value. Conceptually, each property makes a statement about a resource of the form, "The *property_name* of *resource* is *property_value*." For example, "The author of *Moby Dick* is Herman Melville." This statement is represented by metadata in which the resource is the book *Moby Dick*, the property name is *author*, and the property value is *Herman Melville* (see Example 12-2).

Example 12-2. Example XMP

```
<xmp:CreateDate>1851-08-18</xmp:CreateDate>
<xmp:CreatorTool>Ink and Paper</xmp:CreatorTool>
 <dc:creator>
    <rdf:Seq>
       <rdf:li>Herman Melville</rdf:li>
    </rdf:Seq>
```

```
    </dc:creator>
  <dc:title>
      <rdf:Alt>
          <rdf:li xml:lang="x-default">Moby Dick</rdf:li>
      </rdf:Alt>
  </dc:title>
```

All property, structure field, and qualifier names in XMP must be legal XML qualified names. That is, they must be well-formed XML names and in an XML namespace—this applies to top-level properties, struct fields, and qualifiers. This is a requirement inherited from RDF (Resource Definition Framework), the technology on which XMP is based.

Schemas

An XMP Schema is a set of top-level property names in a common XML namespace, along with their data types and descriptive information. Typically, an XMP Schema contains properties that are relevant for particular types of documents or for certain stages of a workflow. There exists a set of standard schemas (*http://adobe.ly/1fNbyyk*), as well as a mechanism for how to define new schemas.

 The term "XMP Schema" is used here to clearly distinguish this concept from other uses of the term "schema," and notably from the W3C XML Schema language. An XMP Schema is typically less formal and defined by documentation instead of a machine-readable schema file.

An XMP Schema is identified by its XML namespace URI. It also has an associated namespace prefix that can take any value, though there are common ones in use. This use of namespaces avoids conflict between properties in different schemas that have the same name but different meanings. For example, two independently designed schemas might have a creator property: in one, it might mean the person who created a resource; and in another, the application used to create the resource.

The term "top-level" distinguishes the root properties in an XMP Schema from the named fields of a structure within a property value. By convention, an XMP Schema defines its top-level properties, but the names of structure fields are part of the data type information.

The data types that can represent the values of XMP properties fall into three basic categories: simple types, structures, and arrays. Since XMP metadata is stored as XML, values of all types are written as Unicode strings. Example 12-3 shows a simple metadata stream.

Example 12-3. An example metadata stream

```
157 0 obj
<<
    /Length 4520
    /Subtype/XML
    /Type/Metadata
>>
stream
<?xpacket begin="Ô ª ø" id="W5M0MpCehiHzreSzNTczkc9d"?>
<x:xmpmeta xmlns:x="adobe:ns:meta/"
 x:xmptk="Adobe XMP Core 5.1-c004 1.136136, 2010/05/14-18:06:40">
    <rdf:RDF xmlns:rdf="http://www.w3.org/1999/02/22-rdf-syntax-ns#">
        <rdf:Description rdf:about=""
                xmlns:xmp="http://ns.adobe.com/xap/1.0/">
            <xmp:ModifyDate>2010-07-06T19:33:16-03:00</xmp:ModifyDate>
            <xmp:CreateDate>2010-07-06T19:33:03-03:00</xmp:CreateDate>
            <xmp:MetadataDate>2010-07-06T19:33:16-03:00</xmp:MetadataDate>
            <xmp:CreatorTool>Acrobat PDFMaker 10.0 for Word</xmp:CreatorTool>
        </rdf:Description>
        <rdf:Description rdf:about=""
xmlns:xmpMM="http://ns.adobe.com/xap/1.0/mm/">
        <xmpMM:DocumentID>uuid:483d2fca-113d-4c81-b650-a39a67866aa6</xmpMM:DocumentID>
        <xmpMM:InstanceID>uuid:83008e27-bcc3-4480-a03a-13dc46d7f1f5</xmpMM:InstanceID>
            <xmpMM:subject>
                <rdf:Seq>
                    <rdf:li>127</rdf:li>
                </rdf:Seq>
            </xmpMM:subject>
        </rdf:Description>
        <rdf:Description rdf:about=""
xmlns:dc="http://purl.org/dc/elements/1.1/">
            <dc:format>application/pdf</dc:format>
            <dc:title>
                <rdf:Alt>
                    <rdf:li xml:lang="x-default">ISO TC 171/SC 2/WG5</rdf:li>
                </rdf:Alt>
            </dc:title>
            <dc:description>
                <rdf:Alt>
                    <rdf:li xml:lang="x-default">ISO/WD 19005-2</rdf:li>
                </rdf:Alt>
            </dc:description>
            <dc:creator>
                <rdf:Seq>
                    <rdf:li>Leonard Rosenthol</rdf:li>
                </rdf:Seq>
            </dc:creator>
        </rdf:Description>
        <rdf:Description rdf:about=""
        xmlns:pdf="http://ns.adobe.com/pdf/1.3/">
            <pdf:Producer>Adobe PDF Library 10.0</pdf:Producer>
        </rdf:Description>
```

```
        <rdf:Description rdf:about=""
  xmlns:pdfx="http://ns.adobe.com/pdfx/1.3/">
          <pdfx:SourceModified>D:20100706222950</pdfx:SourceModified>
          <pdfx:Company>AIIM</pdfx:Company>
          <pdfx:Manager>Betsy Fanning</pdfx:Manager>
        </rdf:Description>
        <rdf:Description rdf:about=""
  xmlns:photoshop="http://ns.adobe.com/photoshop/1.0/">
          <photoshop:headline>
            <rdf:Seq>
              <rdf:li>ISO/WD 19005-2</rdf:li>
            </rdf:Seq>
          </photoshop:headline>
        </rdf:Description>
      </rdf:RDF>
</x:xmpmeta>
<?xpacket end="w"?>
endstream
endobj
```

In this example, you can see the various aspects of XMP that were mentioned previously: RDF, multiple namespaces (dc, xmp, pdf, and xmpMM), and both simple (xmp:Create Date) and array types (dc:creator).

XMP in PDF

The primary metadata stream is for the document itself and is the value of the Metadata entry in the document catalog. In addition, any stream or dictionary object may have metadata attached to it via its Metadata entry. It is recommended that you place the Metadata entry on the dictionary or stream that represents the data itself (such as a font or image).

Along these lines, metadata may also be associated with marked content within a content stream. This association is created by including an entry in the property list dictionary whose key is Metadata and whose value is the metadata stream dictionary (see Example 12-4).

Example 12-4. Example catalog with metadata

```
485 0 obj
<<
    /Type/Catalog
    /Metadata 54 0 R
    /Pages 466 0 R
    /ViewerPreferences<</Direction/L2R>>
>>
endobj

54 0 obj
<<
```

```
    /Type/Metadata
    /Subtype/XML
    /Length 71746
>>
stream
<?xpacket begin="Ôªø" id="W5M0MpCehiHzreSzNTczkc9d"?>
    <x:xmpmeta xmlns:x="adobe:ns:meta/"
                            x:xmptk="Adobe   XMP   Core   5.2-c001   63.139439,
2010/09/27-13:37:26         ">
        <rdf:RDF xmlns:rdf="http://www.w3.org/1999/02/22-rdf-syntax-ns#">
        <rdf:Description rdf:about=""
            xmlns:xmp="http://ns.adobe.com/xap/1.0/">
        <xmp:CreateDate>2011-04-25T15:33:20Z</xmp:CreateDate>
        <xmp:CreatorTool>Microsoft PowerPoint</xmp:CreatorTool>
        <xmp:ModifyDate>2011-04-25T10:34:09-05:00</xmp:ModifyDate>
        <xmp:MetadataDate>2011-04-25T10:34:09-05:00</xmp:MetadataDate>
        </rdf:Description>
        <rdf:Description rdf:about=""
                        xmlns:pdf="http://ns.adobe.com/pdf/1.3/">
            <pdf:Keywords/>
            <pdf:Producer>Adobe Mac PDF Plug-in</pdf:Producer>
        </rdf:Description>
        <rdf:Description rdf:about=""
                        xmlns:dc="http://purl.org/dc/elements/1.1/">
            <dc:format>application/pdf</dc:format>
            <dc:creator>
                <rdf:Seq>
                    <rdf:li>Rick</rdf:li>
                </rdf:Seq>
            </dc:creator>
            <dc:title>
                <rdf:Alt>
                    <rdf:li xml:lang="x-default">Presentation2.pptx</rdf:li>
                </rdf:Alt>
            </dc:title>
        </rdf:Description>
        <rdf:Description rdf:about=""
                        xmlns:xmpMM="http://ns.adobe.com/xap/1.0/mm/">
         <xmpMM:DocumentID>uuid:51b92418-85ef-f843-ba4d-9c6ea3482287</xmpMM:Documen-
tID>
         <xmpMM:InstanceID>uuid:5506218e-628b-8046-8af4-f2eb28096824</xmpMM:Instan-
ceID>
        </rdf:Description>
        </rdf:RDF>
</x:xmpmeta>
<?xpacket end="w"?>
endstream
endobj
```

XMP versus the Info Dictionary

Although the XMP-based document-level metadata referenced from the document's catalog dictionary is the canonical metadata in the document, it may be superseded by updated metadata in the document information dictionary. This is to handle the case where an older PDF processor updates only the information dictionary.

Both XMP and the information dictionary provide a date stamp. If the date stamp in the XMP is equal to or later than the modification date in the document information dictionary, the XMP metadata is taken as authoritative. If, however, the modification date in the document information dictionary is later than the XMP metadata's date stamp, the information stored in the document information dictionary will override any semantically equivalent items in the XMP metadata.

When you are writing metadata, always use XMP.

What's Next

In this chapter, you learned how to incorporate metadata into a PDF at the document as well as the object level. In the next and final chapter, we will look at how PDF became an international standard, both in its entirety as well as various subsets of its full capabilities.

CHAPTER 13

PDF Standards

Adobe Systems introduced PDF to the world in 1993, including a public specification for the format. However, while many developers were able to create their own tools for reading and writing PDF documents, only Adobe could add or change features in the PDF language itself. Those changes were beneficial to Adobe's business, but not always to various industries and market segments. For this reason, the print industry pursued the idea of developing a subset of PDF that could then be standardized through an international body such as the International Organization for Standardization (ISO) (*http://www.iso.org*). The result of this work, and the first of the subsets, was PDF/X. A few years later a variety of government and business interests came together to produce PDF/A, the PDF subset focused on long-term archiving of PDF documents. It was the very public work on the development of PDF/A that led to other industries working to bring about the other standards listed here.

In 2007, Adobe recognized that it was time for the full PDF specification to be brought to the ISO. This led to the publication of ISO 32000-1, which turned PDF 1.7 into a fully open international standard.

PDF (ISO 32000)

ISO 32000-1 represents the formalization and publication of the complete PDF 1.7 edition of the Adobe PDF Reference (*http://www.adobe.com/devnet/pdf/pdf_refer ence.html*) and an open international standard. The ISO committee (TC171/SC2/WG8) spent many years producing a standard that was technically identical to the previous Adobe PDF 1.7, but had undergone an extensive rewriting process to clarify numerous items. This standard is the foundation for all future generations of PDF standards.

With "Adobe's PDF" now standardized, the next move by the committee was to begin work introducing features that they had been wanting in PDF for years. Some examples include the inclusion of geospatial or GIS data, black point compensation for richer color rendition, and improved tagging and structure. At this time, ISO 32000-2 is under development and due to be published sometime in 2015.

PDF/X (ISO 15930)

The first of the PDF subset standards, PDF/X, focused on the needs of print professionals, graphic designers, and creatives by providing specifications for the creation, viewing, and printing of final print-ready or press-ready pages. PDF/X provides guidelines affecting critical aspects of printing, such as color spaces, font embedding, and the use of trapping. It also restricts other content—such as embedded multimedia—that does not directly serve high-quality print production output.

PDF/X-1a (ISO 15930-1), the first of the family, was published in 2001. It specified a subset of PDF that required that all fonts were embedded, no annotations were included, and the only colorspaces allowed to be used were `DeviceCMYK`, `DeviceGray`, and `Sepa ration`. It also required that the file specify whether it has been trapped or not. In 2002, PDF/X-3 (ISO 15930-3) was introduced; it built on PDF/X-1a but allowed for color-managed colors via colorspaces such as `ICCBased` and `Lab`. These original versions of PDF/X-1a and PDF/X-3 were based on PDF 1.3. In 2003 there were updates to both PDF/X-1a (15930-4) and PDF/X-3 (15930-6), that brought them in line with PDF 1.4, but they continued to disallow transparency.

It took a while for the print industry to understand the benefits of and concerns about the use of transparency in PDF, so it wasn't until 2008 that the first version of PDF/X-4 (ISO 15930-7) was published. The version brought PDF/X-3's color-managed model for PDF to a version of PDF (1.6) incorporating transparency, better compression (e.g., JPEG2000 and ObjectStream; see "Cross-reference table" on page 16), and more. However, a few issues were discovered in that original 2008 release, and it was superseded by an update in 2010.

PDF/X-1a, PDF/X-3, and PDF/X-4 all represent completely self-contained files. All fonts, colorspaces, and images must be inside the PDF—no external references are allowed. While that is certainly the normal case for printing, there are situations where the ability to refer to external content or external resources can be beneficial, such as in the variable and transactional data worlds. For those industries, PDF/X-5 (ISO 15930-8) was created to provide a standard that enables either single files or sets of multiple files utilizing external references.

 There was also a PDF/X-2 (ISO 15930-2), which attempted to provide a method for handling external content. Unfortunately, the design was quite poor and it was never publicly implemented. So the industry pretends it never happened!

PDF/A (ISO 19005)

In 2003, representatives from the US government approached Adobe Systems about their need to create a subset of PDF that would be more reliable and consistent than what PDF producers were generating at the time. They needed this reliability to be able to properly maintain PDF documents in their archives for 10, 20, 50, or more years.

PDF/A-1, published in 2005 and based on PDF 1.4, represents a standard for the creation, viewing, and printing of digital documents for the purpose of long-term preservation. These documents are completely self-contained with embedded fonts and consistent color, and without any encryption, enabling them to serve as final documents of record. No references to external content are allowed since those items may not exist in the future. In addition, XMP-based metadata is required to ensure that the file is self-describing (see "XMP" on page 179).

PDF/A-2, published in 2010 and based on PDF 1.7 (ISO 32000-1), brings with it many requested capabilities such as transparency and improved compression utilizing JPEG2000 and object streams. By using ISO 32000-1 as the base standard, PDF/A-2 became the first PDF subset standard to be entirely ISO-based. One feature that was requested by many, but did not make it into PDF/A-2, was the ability to have arbitrary attachments, such as XML data. In order to provide a solution for those workflows, the committee (ISO TC171/SC2/WG5) produced PDF/A-3 in 2012.

Each of the PDF/A standards comes in at least two conformance levels, *a* and *b*. The *a* conformance level can be thought of as the "all" or "accessible" level, as it requires conformance with the complete set of requirements for the standard, including that the file be tagged and structured for accessibility (see Chapter 11 for details). The *b*, or "basic," level of conformance is commonly used by simpler content such as scanned documents or documents whose original digital source is no longer available. PDF/A-2 and PDF/A-3 introduced a third conformance level that can be seen as being in between the others: level *u*, for "Unicode." It requires that all text in the file can be mapped to Unicode (*http://www.unicode.org/versions/Unicode6.2.0/*).

PDF/E (ISO 24517)

Although PDF had seen some basic usage in the engineering market all along, the introduction of support for optional content, 3D, and measurements caused a significant uptake of the format amongst architects, engineers, construction professionals, and product manufacturing teams.

PDF/E was a direct result of the engineering community's desire for a specification that built on top of PDF/A. It focuses on their needs around the exchange of documentation and drawings in the supply chain for document sharing or streamlined review and markup. It specifies requirements for PDF that make it more suitable for building, manufacturing, and geospatial workflows by supporting interactive media, animation, and 3D. Because one of the key use cases for the standard was to enable sharing of content, it allows for the use of encryption and digital rights management.

Published in 2007, PDF/E-1 is based on PDF 1.6. PDF/E-2, which is under development by ISO TC171/SC2/WG7, is expected to be published in 2014 and will be based on ISO 32000-2.

PDF/VT (ISO 16612-2)

While PDF/X-4 and PDF/X-5 address the majority of the print production industry's needs, those working with variable and transactional printing needed some specific additions. In their high-volume workflows involving bank statements and business invoices, the inclusion of rich metadata and identifiable document parts was a necessity. In addition, many parts of these documents are reused, and an optimal way to identify them and reuse them in the printing process was required. PDF/VT, which is based on PDF/X, was published in 2010 and addressed these needs.

There are three flavors of PDF/VT. PDF/VT-1 is a completely self-contained file format based on PDF/X-4, while PDF/VT-2 allows for individual form XObjects to be referenced in other files and is built on PDF/X-5. There is also a special case of PDF/VT-2 called PDF/VT-2s that can be driven entirely in a stream, rather than requiring actual writing to files.

PDF/UA (ISO 14289)

Many governments around the world have laws that require that their publications be accessible to all of their people, regardless of any disabilities they may possess. PDF has long had features (especially via tagging and structure) that enable any document to comply with the general-purpose international accessibility standards, but until recently no PDF-focused standard existed to give concrete direction.

PDF/UA-1, published in 2012, is based on ISO 32000-1 and provides a set of guidelines for creating PDF files that are universally accessible and thus more readable for people with disabilities such as vision impairment or limited mobility.

Other PDF-Related Standards

There are a few other PDF-related standards to be aware of.

PAdES (ETSI TS 102 778)

The European Union (EU) has long been a strong proponent of digital or electronic signatures, including the standardization of signatures based on other serializations such as CMS (CAdES) and XML (XAdES).

In 2008, the European Telecommunications Standards Institute (ETSI) published ETSI 102778, which builds upon the ISO 32000-1 standard to facilitate more secure paperless business transactions. This standard defines a series of profiles for PAdES (PDF Advanced Electronic Signatures) that comply with European Directive 1999/93/EC.

PDF Healthcare

While not a file format standard, the PDF Healthcare (*http://bit.ly/1dO7mwz*) initiative provides best practices and implementation guidelines to facilitate the capture, exchange, preservation, and protection of healthcare information. Following these guidelines provides a more secure electronic container that can store and transmit health-related information including personal documents, XML data, DICOM images and data, clinical notes, lab reports, electronic forms, scanned images, photographs, digital x-rays, and ECGs.

Index

Symbols

(number) sign, 3
% percent sign, 15
() parentheses
    string objects and, 4
    unbalanced, literal strings and, 4
0Ah character, 14
0Dh character, 14
3D, 145–149
    markup dictionaries, 148
    markups, 148
    streams, 147
    view dictionary, 146
    views, 146
3D annotations, 145–149
    dictionary, 146
    streams, 147
<< double angle brackets, 6
<> angle brackets, 4
[] square brackets, 5
\ backslash, 4
\ddd notation, 4

A

AcroForms, 105–122
    field classes, 109–119
    field dictionary, 106–109
    form actions, 119–122

    interactive form dictionary, 105
actions, 79–82
    dictionary, 79
    GoTo, 79
    GoToE, 133
    GoToR, 81
    ImportData action, 122
    launch, 81
    movie, 141
    multimedia, 82
    nested, 82
    rendition, 142–145
    ResetForm, 121
    ResetForm action, 121
    sound, 138
    SubmitForm, 120–121
    URI, 80
Adobe Systems, 185
AIFF format, 137
animation, playing, 139
annotation dictionary, 87
    3D markup and, 148
    widget annotation and, 108
annotations, 87–103
    appearance streams, 88
    circle, 92
    color of, 89
    dictionaries, 87
    drawing markup, 91–100

We'd like to hear your suggestions for improving our indexes. Send email to index@oreilly.com.

About the Author

Leonard Rosenthol is a Principal Scientist and PDF Architect for Adobe Systems, having been involved with PDF technology for more than 15 years. He represents Adobe on various international standards bodies, including the ISO (where he is the Project Editor for PDF/A and PDF/E), W3C, and ETSI/ESI (where he authored the PDF Electronic Signature standard, PAdES). Prior to rejoining Adobe in 2006, Leonard worked as the Director of Software Development for Appligent and as the Chief Innovation Officer for Apago, while also running the successful consulting business of PDF Sages. Before becoming involved in PDF, Leonard was the Director of Advanced Technology for Aladdin Systems and responsible for the development of the StuffIt line of products.

Colophon

The animal on the cover of *Developing with PDF* is a Chilean Plantcutter (*Phytotoma rara*). Also known as the Rufous-tailed Plantcutter, this small species of bird lives primarily in the scrublands, forests, and river valleys of Chile and western Argentina (and has been sighted on the Falkland Islands). The bird gets its name from the special serrated edge on its beak, which allows it to strip off buds, leaves, and fruits from plants. Although primarily herbivorous, Plantcutters will eat insects when necessary and use them as food for their chicks. These birds do not tend to flock; they are commonly seen either singly or in pairs. All species of Plantcutter are sexually dimorphic, which means that the males and females have obviously different observable characteristics. While males have a distinctly reddish brown underside with black and white wings, females have beige undersides and wings, and may have a red throat and forehead. After a mating pair builds a nest out of root fibers, the female lays two to four blue-spotted eggs at a time. The population of Chilean Plantcutters is large and stable, but other species of this bird have not been so lucky. The Peruvian Plantcutter in particular has suffered a great deal from habitat destruction. It has been classified as endangered as coastal Peruvian forests have been increasingly converted to farmland, displacing the birds and causing a sharp decline in population. Conservation efforts are underway, but it remains unclear whether the Peruvian Plantcutter will ever enjoy the same success that its Chilean cousin does.

The cover image is from Wood's *Animate Creations*. The cover fonts are URW Typewriter and Guardian Sans. The text font is Adobe Minion Pro; the heading font is Adobe Myriad Condensed; and the code font is Dalton Maag's Ubuntu Mono.

Get even more for your money.

Have it your way.

CPSIA information can be obtained at www.ICGtesting.com
Printed in the USA
LVOW03s2350020314

375771LV00008B/11/P